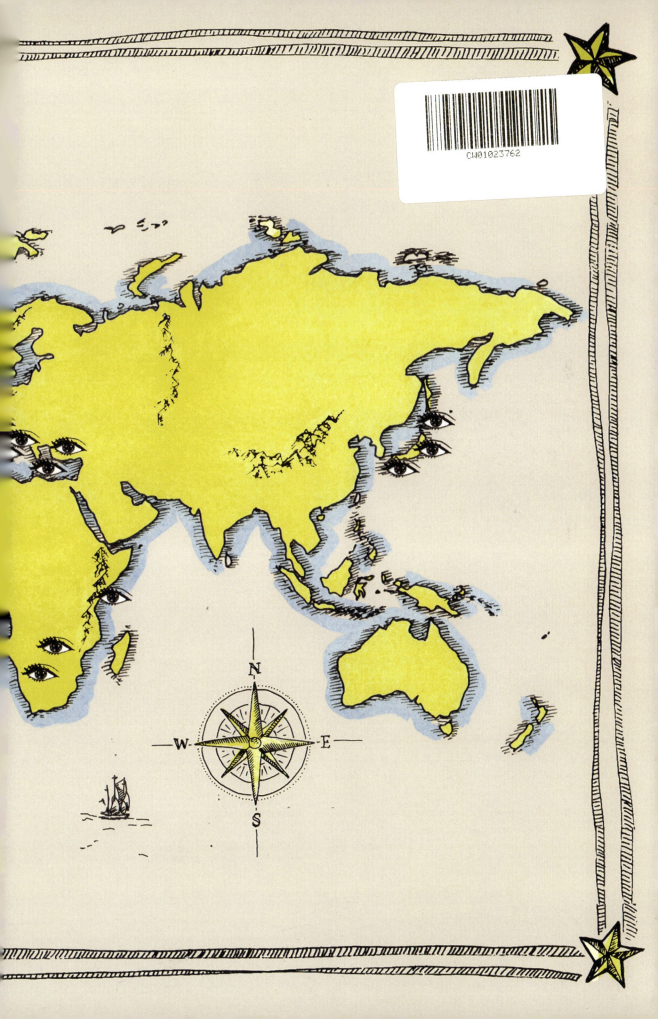

Travels with Chufy

This book is dedicated to my mother,
Maita Barrenechea, who taught me to explore the world
with curiosity and tireless thirst,
and to my husband, Alex de Betak,
who supports my dreams wherever they take us.

Front cover: Horseback riding in the sea,
Harbour Island, Bahamas. © Alexandre de Betak.
Back cover: Lunch on a hanging bridge over
the River Traful, Patagonia. © Isaias Miciu.
Endpages: A map of @Chufy's travel destinations.
© Lucia Sanchez Barrenechea.

© 2017 Assouline Publishing
3 Park Avenue, 27th Floor
New York, NY 10016, USA
Tel.: 212-989-6769 Fax: 212-647-0005
assouline.com

Creative Direction: Camille Dubois
Design: Paola Nauges
Editorial direction: Esther Kremer
Editor: Lindsey Tulloch
Photo editor: Hannah Hayden
Color separation by AltaImage
Printed in China
ISBN: 9781614285939

All rights reserved.
No part of this publication may
be reproduced or transmitted
in any form or by any means,
electronic or otherwise, without
prior consent of the publisher.

SOFÍA SANCHEZ
DE BETAK

Travels with Chufy

ASSOULINE

6   INTRODUCTION

10   NAPLES, ITALY | Albergo del Purgatorio

18   KASTELLORIZO, GREECE | Mediterraneo Megisti

26   KYOTO, JAPAN | Tawara-ya Ryokan

32   POSCHIAVO, SWITZERLAND | La Rösa

38   PATAGONIA, ARGENTINA | Estancia Arroyo Verde

46   MARRAKECH, MOROCCO | Riad Jardin Secret

52   FLATEY, ICELAND | Hótel Flatey

58   KIWAYU, KENYA | Mike's Camp

68   RHODES, GREECE | Marco Polo Mansion

80   UWAJIMA, SHIKOKU, JAPAN | Kiya Ryokan

84   HARBOUR ISLAND, BAHAMAS | Ocean View Club

94   MÉRIDA, MEXICO Hacienda | Santa Rosa

100   MAKGADIKGADI PAN, BOTSWANA | Jack's Camp

110   ENTRE RÍOS, ARGENTINA | Los Ombues Lodge

116   TRANCOSO, BRASIL | Uxua

124   MALLORCA, SPAIN | Sa Palosa

130   GARZÓN, URUGUAY | Casa Anna

134   POSITANO, ITALY | Villa TreVille

144   MENDOZA, ARGENTINA | Finca Los Alamos

150   PATMOS, GREECE | Archontariki

156   LAIKIPIA, KENYA | Ol Malo

164   TOKYO, JAPAN | Caravan Tokyo

168   ISTANBUL, TURKEY | Hazz

178   PUGLIA, ITALY | Masseria Potenti

186   DIRECTORY

192   ACKNOWLEDGMENTS & CREDITS

INTRODUCTION

There are countless ways to travel, and I—born to a globe-trotting family in Argentina and sustaining a fashion career rooted in images in Paris and New York—have experimented with many of them. From backpacking distant mountains to cruising aboard decadent yachts, from staying in ultra-modern thousand-room skyscrapers to volunteering in camps, I have learned one thing: Even the highest star ratings can fade. Despite the refined touches some hotels may have, the repetitive litany of amenities and services start to blend in after a while, as do my memories of staying there. I am constantly compelled to seek new wellsprings of creativity, and it is always travel that resonates most deeply with me.

Whether you are visiting a major metropolis or venturing to the more remote parts of the world, where you stay and who you meet profoundly shape your experience of that place. Have you ever stayed at an unconventional hotel deeply buried in the jungle or in a city's maze? Ate in a fisherman's shack worthy of Michelin stars? Stayed up until dawn listening to a host's tales of discovery? Or found hidden treasures in a shop with no sign on the door? Looking beyond the glossy veneer of obvious travel tips is something I have been trained to do from a young age, thanks to parents and grandparents who sparked within me a relentless craving for adventure. Growing up, I would be delighted to hear their stories, which spanned continents, each tale another assurance that there is no better way to learn than by air, land, or sea.

I love taking pictures as much as I love leaving my camera and phone back in the room. These are two different ways of discovering a place: through a lens or with my own eyes.

My parents have worked in the travel industry since before I can remember, from the days when Argentina was barely a blip on the map for most travelers and there were hardly any hotels beyond the city limits of Buenos Aires. Regardless, we would travel all around, staying at our family's or our friends' estancias instead. Toward the end of the twentieth century, when these massive estates struggled to remain in one piece, my mother persuaded many of her friends to open their doors and welcome travelers as a way to sustain their properties. It was a radical concept at the time for prestigious families to host strangers at their grand and remote estancias, but just like in Europe and other parts of the world, it was a natural evolution. It became a win-win for everyone involved: The estate owners found a new way to preserve their slices of paradise while making friends from all over the world, and it allowed for people to visit new parts of Argentina that had previously been inaccessible and experience the country like some very fortunate locals.

ABOVE: At Palacio Santa Cándida in Argentina with my mother, Maita, and my sisters, Lucia and Catalina.
OPPOSITE: Discovering the charms of Patagonia from a very young age.

Today, my unending quest for inspiration has brought me from the most distant plains of South America to the untamed jungle coasts of Africa to secret hideaways deep within the little streets of Istanbul. Venturing out into the world—armed with little more than a carry-on, a camera, and a fiery passion for exploration—I have discovered that there is nothing I love better than getting lost in translation and translating my way out. Traversing countries, meeting inspiring people, and exploring new places that change my view of the world is beyond compare. And wherever I go, my search remains the same—for the spots that strike a balance between refinement, quality, and sense of place; the ones that have little regard for the scale of traditional luxury ratings; the places that feel right. This book is a collection of those I have found all around the world, following these criteria embedded in me, whether they are far-off destinations or just hidden spots in already familiar locales.

There is an excess of options and information out in the world, but very little has been curated. Even my closest friends tend to love the exact opposite things I do. So after years of careful listening—learning whose advice to follow, when to take notes, and when to immediately book a ticket—I have created this book, highlighting the places that, to me, have the perfect balance between luxury and simplicity, coziness and history, fascinating hosts and privacy: in summary, luxury beyond stars.

NAPLES, ITALY
ALBERGO DEL PURGATORIO

THE DISCOVERY

"A friend insisted that I swing through Naples during a recent trip to Italy, promising that I'd never regret staying at the secret guesthouse Albergo del Purgatorio. She told us about its story, philosophy, and enigmatic hostess Nathalie de Saint Phalle (a bohemian aristocrat from Paris), and I was captivated right away. The palazzo is incredible in its decadence and faded grandeur—our "room" was the entire upstairs apartment, with lofty ceilings covered in contemporary art, books all over the place, a bright red bathroom, and windows facing a courtyard where Italian women spoke to one another. The minute I arrived, I understood the magic of Naples."

THE DESTINATION

"I give strangers the keys to a house full of art and my personal things," says Nathalie de Saint Phalle, the visionary behind this boho *hôtel particulier* in Naples's Palazzo Spinelli. A former journalist, rug importer, book collector, and aesthete, de Saint Phalle opened up the palazzo overlooking the Via dei Tribunali to guests in the late nineties as a guesthouse for friends, off-the-beaten-path travelers, and passersby with a story to tell. She settled in the City of the Sun by chance in 1991, after she'd become disenchanted by the French literati and decided to head to southern Italy in search of a radical, vibrant community of authors and artists. She found it in Naples and soon realized that the best way to capture the city's creative electricity is by giving it an eccentric home.

The buildings comprising the Purgatorio, as it is known today, date back to the fourteenth and sixteenth centuries, but it wasn't until the front palazzo's construction in the seventeenth century that they were unified as a single structure. Today, that palazzo is as decadent and dreamlike as it is discreet: Twelve weather-worn Greek statues loom above a vast interior elliptical courtyard—the only one of its kind in Naples, and one of the only ones left in the world—which leads to a quiet two-storied entrance hall where an elegant double-sided staircase loops splendidly up to a maze of rooms. Prints and

The circular palazzo at the entrance to the Purgatorio dates back to the Renaissance and is one of the last of its kind still standing.

The grand staircase at the entrance to your home in Naples.

Incredibly tall ceilings covered in art from Robert Kaplan's friends.

photographs cover the vibrantly painted walls, bright tapestry and carpets culled from de Saint Phalle's extensive travels (in Egypt, Turkey, and Yemen, to list just a few), and thousands of books that teeter in stacks on tabletops and in drawers, along windowsills and across makeshift shelves on floors. There is a pastiche of quirky bric-a-brac souvenirs including Noguchi lamps and objects by designers from Philippe Starck to Christophe Pillet.

"I've traveled so much in my life and was always staying in the houses of others," Nathalie explains. "A home should be a self-portrait, with a constellation of personal things that tells the story of its owner. But at the Purgatorio, I also wanted to experiment with that idea and put a spin on that concept by inventing the home of somebody else." De Saint Phalle has filled the residence with friends of friends and out-of-town visitors for the past twenty-five years: Guests are invited to stay in the rooms of her personal apartment, where the furniture and art is eclectic in provenance and design, from collages of her father, the Beat poet Bernard Heidsieck, to Tsé & Tsé dishes and mismatched China plates. But the grandest set of rooms, all done in deep reds and plush fabrics, belongs to the elusive Robert Kaplan, an imaginary art collector that de Saint Phalle has dreamed up as the fictional proprietor of the Purgatorio. Named after Cary Grant's character in Alfred Hitchcock's *North by Northwest*, he is but one of the many narrative twists that she has invented to inspire mystery and incite conversation.

Each guest is asked to leave a book of his or her choosing upon departure, and the resulting library—buoyant with novels, essays, journals, and poetry volumes in countless different languages and translations—is a literary imprint and legacy of everyone who has passed through its halls and slept among its colorful quarters.

DON'T MISS

Get custom shirts at the old-school tailor and shirtmaker Camiceria Piccolo; coffee at the nearest bar (there is no better coffee than Neapolitan coffee) or out on the terrace at Piazza San Domenico Maggiore; the pizza at Di Matteo; ice cream at Gay Odin; a stroll through the narrow *vicoli* (alleys) of the old city; dinner at Da Dora for some fresh fish among the locals; shopping for shoes at Poggioreale, the Sunday morning market; a day trip to Pompeii at dusk to explore the ruins without any crowds.

Nathalie put together a few books with all the stories and photographs guests have sent her about Mr. Kaplan.

KASTELLORIZO, GREECE
MEDITERRANEO MEGISTI

THE DISCOVERY

"Getting to the Greek island of Kastellorizo is an odyssey of sorts, to say the least. There is only one tiny airport, and it just might be the smallest in the world. The tarmac (if it can even be called that) is so short and narrow that planes have no room for error, and there are also no lights on the runway, meaning that planes can't land after dark. If the conditions are anything but just right, a plane will not even be able to land, and sometimes people wait days to leave! And should visitors have the good fortune to land on the island, another challenge awaits them: There is only one taxi, so one must patiently wait in line to leave the airport. If simply accessing Kastellorizo is a test of patience, I like to think that destiny allows only the people who are meant to be here to complete the journey. It is a captivating place, once travelers are lucky enough to complete the trip."

THE DESTINATION

Kastellorizo is one of the most remote Greek islands, actually much nearer to Turkey in both geography and influence. Whereas the more touristic islands like Santorini and Mykonos, which are much closer to mainland Greece, are built in the classic blue-and-white color scheme, Kastellorizo exudes multiple colors and Anatolian style. Since antiquity, it has always been a stopover island as opposed to a destination—there are ancient inscriptions all over the island pointing the way to the much-larger Rhodes—because only those who appreciate its quiet, slow-paced charms are intrigued and ultimately rewarded by staying here.

The Mediterraneo Megisti boasts beautiful views of the water and charming town.

Renting a boat and going for a private dive is always a plus!

On the advice of a trusted friend, I stayed at the Mediterraneo Megisiti, an ancient mansion that stands gracefully over the water, overlooking the quays of this port town. The rooms are colorful and comfortable, and the hues of the walls come to life every morning as the warm sunrise peeks over the sea and through the windows. It was easy to fall in love with a place like this, but it was the woman who owns the Mediterraneo who became one of the greatest finds in all my travels.

Former Parisian architect Marie Rivalant is a woman of many smiles, and she jokes that Kastellorizo made her fall in love three times: with the island itself (where she now resides), with a man living there (whom she ended up marrying), and then with an old mansion on the water (which, luckily, she acquired and turned into this elegant retreat). Moving to Kastellorizo has brought out Marie's relaxed side, but she is still a Parisian woman of rned taste at heart. She sits down with all her guests and provides suggestions of what to do on the island. One can visit the Mediterraneo alone and find a friend in her. For me, I thought it was deeply beautiful and moving to see someone as cosmopolitan as she who left it all behind for love and moved to this very different life in paradise. She was brave to do so, but it shows in her many smiles that it paid off.

DON'T MISS

Shopping for hats, carpets, and towels at Marie's shop; taking a boat to the Turkish market—Marie knows the way—to pick up linens and spices; eating fish, fish, and more fish every day; snacking on the best olives to be found anywhere and picking up a jar to bring home; climbing the nearby mountain and exploring the ruins on the summit, which date back to the fourth century BC; and diving off cliffs into the sea, swimming in crystal-clear waters with rainbow fish darting about, and turning around to this pristine, technicolor town tucked under the mountain.

ABOVE: Marie Rivalant and her husband, Georgios, are the ones to know on the island. They will make you laugh like nobody else!
OPPOSITE: Marie's boutique, Mediterraneo.

A turquoise sea just steps from your front door.

KYOTO, JAPAN
TAWARA-YA RYOKAN

THE DISCOVERY

"As opposed to the pulsing urban sprawl of Tokyo, time appears to stand still in Kyoto. Cherry blossom trees line many of the streets, and there are more gorgeous temples than one could possibly visit in one trip—but it was the first time I came face-to-face with a real-life geisha that I felt absolutely swept away. My heart froze the moment I saw her perfectly powdered ivory skin and scarlet lips, and I instantly understood Kyoto's centuries-old commitment to tradition and elegance."

THE DESTINATION

The best thing about visiting Japan and going outside the megalopolis of Tokyo is the chance to stay in one of its many *ryokan*, a type of traditional inn that originated in the seventeenth century. There are many in Kyoto, but none compare to the Tawara-ya, which, amazingly, is three hundred years old—and, even more amazingly, has been run by the same family since its beginning.

The Tawara-ya's hospitality begins upon arrival. As in any Japanese household, guests must remove their shoes, and there is one staff member whose exclusive job it is to look after everyone's shoes—helping guests step in and out of them, polishing them, drying them if it is raining outside, and making sure each pair is ready when it comes time to leave. After visitors give him their shoes, they can peer around and see that there isn't really a lobby at the Tawara-ya. Another staff member will guide guests quietly to their room, passing through a dim, quiet hallway lit only by ancient-looking lanterns. Open any of the *shoji* sliding doors to see that the decor is an exercise in luxurious restraint, each room lined with tatami mats, light streaming in from its private zen garden. There is an item or two in every single room from the Tawara-ya's extensive collection of priceless antiques and art—one that would rival any museum—and it is said that the owners rotate the pieces through the rooms based on the seasons and the presumed tastes of their guests.

Each sticker is left by a geisha and serves as her calling card. In Japan, if you send a geisha a letter—no address, only her name—she will receive it.

 This attention to every minute detail is a beautiful testament to Kyoto's tradition of hospitality. Any member of the staff will willingly stop what they are doing to offer advice on where to go and what to do in the city, and will happily provide insider tips or help secure a dinner reservation. The family has not run this inn for three centuries without making a few connections in town along the way.

DON'T MISS

Listening to the swaying stalks overhead in the Sagano Bamboo Forest; peeking into the tea houses of the Gion district, where geishas still entertain; an afternoon spent sampling the strange delights and mysterious ingredients at Nishiki Market; getting a geisha makeover and walking around town; bar hopping in Gion—only lucky visitors are let into the bars, and we loved B. B-Peak Snack for some karaoke time with the locals; dancing to Latin music at El Coyote; driving out to Shiga Prefecture, an hour away, for the most incredible pottery shopping; and a moment of quiet meditation at Kinkaku-ji, a stunning temple covered entirely in gold leaf.

It was my second trip to Kyoto, so I decided to skip a few temples and have some fun—we had a head-to-toe geisha and samurai makeover.

ABOVE, TOP: At Matsudaya, a Michelin-starred restaurant, the sushi man told us where he got all of his exquisite pottery—only an hour away from Kyoto, we found pottery paradise. Shiga Prefecture holds all the best ceramic dealers for professionals. We bought about thirty pounds of ceramics and had them shipped straight to New York. They arrived perfectly wrapped with not a scratch just a week later.
ABOVE, BOTTOM AND OPPOSITE: We visited the home and studio of one of Chiso's main artists, who meticulously paints these fabrics for the best kimono haute couture house in Kyoto.

POSCHIAVO, SWITZERLAND
LA RÖSA

THE DISCOVERY

"A romanticized vision of life in the Alps can be found if one knows where to look. High in the mountains somewhere between Switzerland and Italy, far from the urban sprawl of Zürich and beyond the tourism of St. Moritz, there is a small village where wild deer and mountain goats walk through the streets, where locals enjoy a quiet pace of life, and where time stands still."

THE DESTINATION

There is always a slight chill in the air in Poschiavo, partly due to its location. Perched high in the Swiss Alps, the town is surrounded by Italy to both the east and west and Lago di Poschiavo to the south. Poschiavo is probably not the place for people looking for Michelin-star dining or luxurious spa treatments—this is an authentic Swiss border town that time seems to have forgotten, where people come to experience the exquisite vastness and solitude of mountain valleys.

The place to stay in this hidden spot, according to my friends and travel gurus Paola Caroini and Laura Taccari, is La Rösa, a renovated post office and trading station in the center of town. The rooms have been exquisitely converted into elegant bedchambers outfitted with local carved-wood furniture, red-and-white Vichy sheets, folk blankets, and the sweetest flower decorations throughout. Dinner is served family style at a large farm table, with candles and fireplaces as the only sources of light and the aromas of burning wood and freshly baked apple pie lingering on the breeze. Leave the windows open overnight to be awoken by gentle bleating of goats in the barn next door carried over by the crisp alpine air.

DON'T MISS

Hopping aboard the Bernina Express, largely considered the most scenic train ride in the world, which stops in town; an early morning hike over the Bernina Pass; chartering a boat ride across the impossibly placid waters of the Lago di Poschiavo; and a quick visit to the Museo Casa Console, where the sweeping beauty of this region is captured by Swiss artists.

There are thoughtful details in every inch of the house. It feels like the family is still living there!

Growing up as the middle one of three sisters, I always identified with Laura Ingalls Wilder!

PATAGONIA, ARGENTINA
ESTANCIA ARROYO VERDE

THE DISCOVERY

"Every visit to Patagonia feels like a fresh discovery, and I have always felt drawn to the wild heart of this untamed country. My family is very outdoorsy, and we all began fly-fishing in the rivers of Argentina at a very young age. We would always stay at the same place: Estancia Arroyo Verde, the home of my stepdad's family, the Larivières. Meme Larivière, Buby's aunt, has long been my role model. I have never met such an energetic and knowledgeable woman; she's like a grandmother to me, and Arroyo Verde is my dream home. The enchanting house stands on a 10,000-acre estate, where the snowcapped Andes fall into the heart of the steppe, where the idyllic Traful River runs free and the vistas stretch far out into the distance, farther than the eye can see or the mind can even comprehend."

THE DESTINATION

Visiting Estancia Arroyo Verde always reminds me of traveling back in time to the Argentina of the frontier days—gauchos, wide-open pampas, and innumerable adventures. The cozy, light-filled house is full of family heirlooms and old-school charms: rubber waders hanging from stag antlers on the porch, turn-of-the-century English sideboards, faded Patagonian rugs, antique fishing prints, and leather-bound first editions. There are sepia-tinged photographs throughout the house, of noteworthy past guests like President Eisenhower, King Leopold of Belgium, and famous anglers including Mel Krueger and Ernest Schwiebert. Four bedrooms in the main house offer views of English gardens planted with roses, lavender, and foxgloves, but the most idyllic sleeping quarters are about a mile away at the one-bedroom, no-electricity log cabin, which is perched on a rocky promontory overlooking the shimmering turquoise waters and endless unspoiled wilderness of Lake Traful.

I've been diving in Lake Traful since before I can remember. There's nothing like that cold water to wake up all your senses!

This is Charlie, our dog,
who loves Patagonia as much as we do.

What I love the most about staying here is that the Larivières treat all their guests like old friends, not like precious five-star clients—so when it comes time to go horseback riding across the steppe, it's a sure bet that guests will have to learn how to saddle their own horses! It was here that I learned how to ride properly, and I have almost too many fond memories of going for long rides, exploring the wilderness with Meme's daughters and granddaughters.

Meals are enjoyed in large groups, and Meme is known to share the most amusing anecdotes about the estancia's history over hearty homemade dinners: empanadas, *carbonada* served inside a pumpkin, *bifes a la criolla*, and *puchero*, all served with a local Malbec or Meme's signature cocktail, a refreshing Pisco Sour whipped up from scratch every night in the bar. It doesn't take long for the slow, cathartic pace of the estancia to set in—this is a place where idle hours are spent chasing the horizon on horseback with the gauchos, enjoying outdoor picnics on prairies of lupines, and casting for rainbow trout and salmon on the legendary Traful River. One of my favorite things is stargazing under the glittering midnight sky, drinking in the millions of stars surrounded by nothing but the sweeping beauty of the Argentinian wilderness.

DON'T MISS

Saddling a horse, crossing the Traful River, and riding through the lake on horseback; lunch on the estancia's romantic hanging bridge; a visit to Los Cóndores, the nesting site of the majestic Andean condor; and a day trip to Las Mellizas, twin lakes hidden in the mountains, passing by caves with Indian paintings and snorkeling down the river sighting trout and salmon in the crystalline pools.

ABOVE: Meme Larivière and Buby, her nephew, are the soul and spirit of Arroyo Verde.
OPPOSITE, TOP: The cabin hangs over a cliff with stunning views of Lake Traful. It's only you and nature there.

Everyone in my family loves fly-fishing. I never became very good at it, but when I set foot in that river I always get a trout or a salmon!

Alex and I hosted a welcome lunch here for our wedding. There were horses and fly-fishing for the daring ones. The real star of the day was our talented and handsome chef, Francis Mallmann. He prepared sixteen whole lambs and fresh-caught salmon in the traditional *curanto* style—cooked underground for hours.
BELOW: My mother, Maita, and my stepfather, Buby, with whom I visit Patagonia every year.

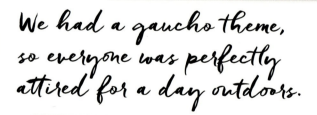

We had a gaucho theme, so everyone was perfectly attired for a day outdoors.

Lunch on a hanging bridge over the River Traful.

MARRAKECH, MOROCCO
RIAD JARDIN SECRET

THE DISCOVERY

"Upon arrival in Marrakech, travelers are confronted by a loud, hectic city where ancient and modern worlds exist side by side. This is not the easiest place to understand—if the meandering, narrow alleyways of the Medina are any indication, this is a place filled with unknown truths just beyond one's grasp. To my good fortune, a few friends referred me to Riad Jardin Secret—precisely the kind of place to help me experience Marrakech for all its decadence and mystery."

THE DESTINATION

Riad Jardin Secret has been given a second lease on life by creative duo Cyrielle and Julien. Both Parisians at heart, Cyrielle used to be a model and photographer, while Julien worked as a style expert before becoming a creative force behind young luxury labels. Craving adventure and a profound change of lifestyle, the duo chose to settle in Marrakech after their many visits there.

Black-and-white photos and artisanal decorative objects dialogue with the magnificent Zellige tilework and *tadelakt* walls. The organic forms and simple design chosen reflect a sense of Moroccan history, inspired by the "anti-modern" way of life.

The riad's name is no accident: The address is whispered among the initiated like a best-kept secret. To gain access, one must be in the know.

Legend has it that the secret garden was the folly of a rich Marrakechi who built two almost identical riads side by side to house his lovers. One of the women was his favorite, and he dedicated this beautiful setting to hiding the immense love he had for her.

A peaceful retreat set apart from the bustling city.

DON'T MISS

Escaping the hot midday sun with a leisurely lunch at the riad, where diners must try the homemade couscous; shopping for the finest linens, velvet Morrocan coats, and shoes at Beldi; stopping by La Mamounia for a drink at the jazzy Churchill Bar and being teleported to the 1920s; taking the time to enjoy an incredible breakfast feast; following a lantern-carrying guide through the mazelike alleys of the Medina to have dinner at Le Foundouk; and grabbing a drink at the Grand Café de la Poste, which evokes cinematic 1920s Morocco with its potted palms, wicker chairs, and immaculate white linens. And of course, don't leave town before taking a nighttime stroll through the Jemaa el Fna, where visitors will be delighted with games, fortune-tellers, snake charmers, and musicians.

This is the kind of thing I buy on trips but never wear until a decade later....

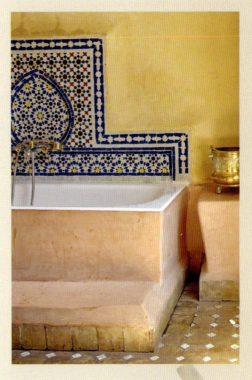

FLATEY, ICELAND
HÓTEL FLATEY

THE DISCOVERY

"There are no cars allowed on the island of Flatey, which only adds to this pristine hideaway's supreme sense of tranquility. The island itself is located off the northwest coast of Iceland, tucked in an ancient glacial bay and accessible only by ferry. We visited in midsummer, where the daylight is almost endless, and the sun sets for barely two hours. Puffins chirp and glide down the rocky shoreline, the architecture of the twenty or so houses is simple yet cheerful and colorful, and gloomy ancient shipwrecks dot the beach. At first glimpse, there is a quietness to Flatey that makes this place feel profoundly still and perhaps a little spooky. But as I walked along the water under the midnight sun, everything bathed in warm pastel twilight, I caught shimmering glimpses of the island's quirky personality."

THE DESTINATION

Despite being settled since the twelfth century, Flatey has remained whisper-quiet. Perhaps that is because the earliest inhabitants were monks. Today, the island is only inhabited during the summer months, and during the winters it is rumored that the population drops down to five inhabitants. Guests do not come to Flatey for obvious luxury—they come for the luxury of solitude and peace.

There is only one place to stay on the island: the Hótel Flatey. Comprising a series of buildings wrapped around the town square, the place feels more like a home than a hotel. When guests aren't out exploring the island, they lounge in the wood-paneled parlor, which is filled with books and games. Built in classic stark-yet-quirky Icelandic style,

the bedrooms have pale, colorful walls and impossibly crisp white sheets. Each room key is adorned with a different bird charm because, as I came to discover, the island is a rich destination for bird-watching.

One evening, after a long walk around the island trying to spy some birds myself (not that I am an expert by any means, but you never know), I found myself back in the middle of the town square. I peeked through the front doors of the little church and was totally awestruck. There at the altar stood an elderly couple in matching Icelandic sweaters—having been married for decades, they were renewing their vows. For a place with such an austere, cold appearance, I felt like I had stumbled, even if for just an instant, across a tender moment of incredible warmth. It might be a tiny island, I thought, but Flatey is a place with immense soul.

DON'T MISS

Visit in summer for the most agreeable weather and late-night twilights that last for hours. Bird-watching and long walks by the water are a must. Convince a local fisherman to take a trip to the secret hot springs in the middle of the nearby sea. Don't leave without trying the Hótel's traditional yet unpretentious Icelandic cuisine—I loved the impossibly fresh pink caviar and blueberry lamb. And, of course, pick up a traditional Icelandic sweater to bring home.

ABOVE: Puffins are everywhere on the island—even on the room keys.

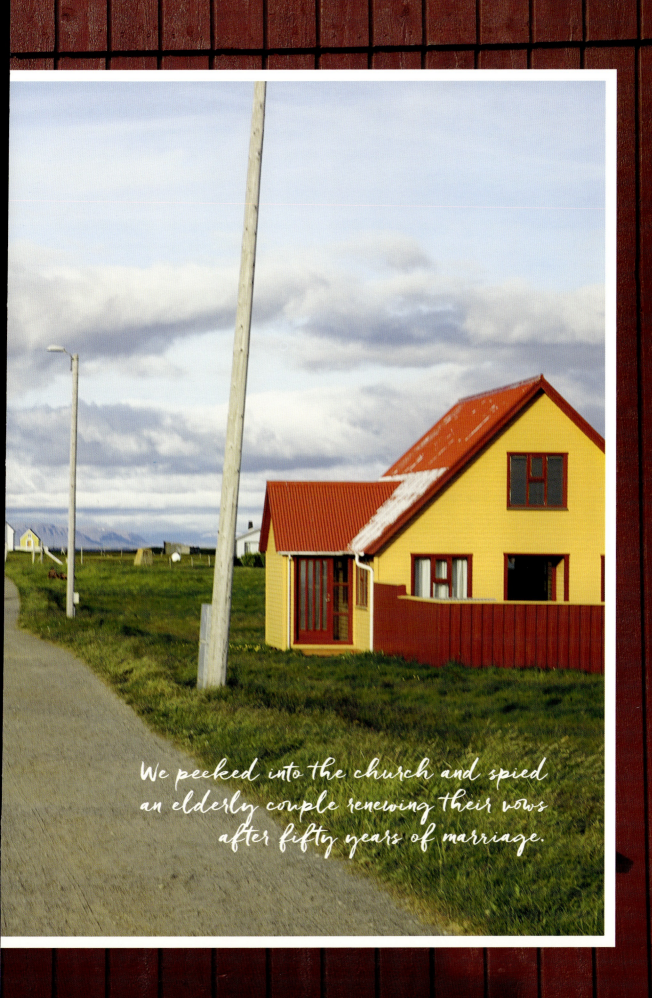

We peeked into the church and spied an elderly couple renewing their vows after fifty years of marriage.

KIWAYU, KENYA

MIKE'S CAMP

THE DISCOVERY

"We arrived at Mike's Camp on Kiwayu island by boat, about an hour's ride from Kenya's Lamu airport. So by the time I had flown halfway around the globe to Nairobi, flown again to the regional airport, and then taken a boat across the water and then through a labyrinthine forest of mangrove trees, I felt like a real-life Robinson Crusoe, marooned in a completely hidden part of the world. Several close friends whose taste I deeply admire have all, at one point or another, spent time as elegant castaways at Mike's Camp, and I was keen to discover what they'd found in this remote place. And then, as our boat emerged from the mangroves, I saw a small but gorgeous pier. Standing at the end of it was Mike himself, smiling and waiting to welcome us. I was ready for adventure."

THE DESTINATION

There are only a few people in the world who can pull off going by a single name, but Mike is one of them. His complete backstory is a long, winding narrative that gives new meaning to the expression "truth is stranger than fiction." I won't try and do it justice here, but just as a taste: It goes from his years working in the oil industry, to sinking a Jeep in the Dodori River, to exploring the ancient Lamu Archipelago on a dhow, to a couple of nights in jail on the Somalian border. Imagine!

OPPOSITE, TOP: When the tide is low, airplanes can land directly on the sand out front.

All the structures were built by hand with help from the locals. In their imperfections lies their beauty.

The unabridged version of Mike's story is best told by Mike himself over late-night drinks, but the most important part is that in 1992 he built Mike's Camp, a hidden destination on a remote stretch of Kiwayu's shore. The camp was built in tandem with some of the local people, and the compound is now a series of huts scattered among Kiwayu's mangroves and beaches. Each guest hut is deliciously large and open to nature, with elegant locally made furniture and vibrant tie-dyed pillows strewn everywhere. Days in Kenya can be oppressively hot, so it is important to fill the morning with activities like sailing and snorkeling before the midday sun gets too strong. Luckily, each room is outfitted with hammocks and daybeds that make for wonderful afternoon naps.

Mike was the ultimate host—his pancake recipe alone is worth flying to Kenya. He also knew so much! He could easily speak at length about every star, every bug, and every person who worked for him. He was always very helpful and generous with his time, teaching us how to use his sand yacht and how to fish for oysters. I heard from a friend that when dinners at Mike's Camp get boring, he goes under the table and bites everyone's ankles—fortunately, that did not happen to us! The camp itself is not luxurious by way of amenities (it was here that I first learned how to take a bucket shower); but rather, it is about experiencing a part of the world so remote and pristine that, if only for a few nights, guests feel like explorers on a once-in-a-lifetime journey.

DON'T MISS

Travelers who time their arrival with low tide can actually fly to Mike's Camp, landing right on the sand. Work up an appetite with sailing, wakeboarding, snorkeling, and boogie boarding in the morning, then harvest oysters all afternoon and eat them straight from the shell. At night, walk down to the beach to gaze at the millions of glimmering stars in the inky sky overhead. Mike truly knows the secrets behind every corner of this tiny island—if it's the right time of year, ask him to point out the secret spot where baby turtles hatch and crawl into the sea.

We happened to be the only guests in Kiwayu in the entire month of August. We had ten miles of pristine beach all to ourselves!

Make sure to ask Mike to show you the secret spot where you can find fresh oysters.

Kiwayu is a long, thin island about ten miles long, but only a five-minute walk across. It is a gorgeous place where the sun rises on one side over the Indian Ocean, then sets on the other side over dense mangrove islands.

RHODES, GREECE
MARCO POLO MANSION

THE DISCOVERY

"Rhodes has the entirely unfair reputation of being a tourist trap for big cruise ships and party people, many of whom prefer hanging out at the bars rather than exploring the island's rich cultural and architectural offerings. The main streets in town are choked with souvenir shops and tourists, but just a few minutes' walk out of the chaos, I began to feel entirely transported. The Marco Polo Mansion, which is actually a gracious garden-level restaurant with a few private guest rooms scattered around the upper floors, was on a hushed side street. As I stood in front of the doors of this perfectly gracious medieval home, I saw the frenetic, crowded scene three blocks to my left—and to my right was an impeccable ancient city, unspoiled by tourism and inviting my discovery. It was then that I knew there was much more to Rhodes than meets the eye."

THE DESTINATION

As a city, Rhodes was fortified successively by the Greeks, Romans, Byzantines, and Knights of St. John, and then the Ottomans. The city itself is remarkably preserved, and I was utterly enchanted to spend hours wandering its streets admiring the centuries of architectural and artistic influences. It is no wonder, then, that the island came highly referred from no fewer than three of my most trusted friends. Jeweler Elie Top, designer Vincent Darré, and photographer François Halard are three men of the utmost discerning standards, whose taste I trust immensely. They knew that beyond the obvious, tourist-laden center of town, Rhodes is a deeply enchanting place with manifold mysteries to offer. All three also knew that the Marco Polo is the secret to unlocking Rhodes.

You can arrive on Rhodes by either boat or plane. After you get into the old city, you need to walk through narrow medieval streets to reach this fascinating place, known as a restaurant with a few rooms for guests. There's a small door with no extravagant sign or elegant entrance, but from the moment you set foot in your temporary home, everything is grandiose.

Just beyond the Marco Polo's entrance is a silent garden shaded by centuries-old walls. Enter, and not even the already quiet street on which the house sits can be heard from inside. The only sounds here come when the neighbors next door talk to each other from window to window. But as opposed to the loud shouts of the tourists in town, the voices of the hotel's neighbors feel hushed, familiar, and almost blended in like white noise. The rooms are luxurious, but in a very unpretentious way—the beds are tall and delicate, the carpets exquisite, and the ambiance perfectly styled. Every room has its own color, and all are perfectly matched. Impossibly cozy, plush daybeds are draped with featherweight linens, and overstuffed pillows spill in piles onto the floors. The smell of garlic and baking bread floats on the breeze through open windows. The Marco Polo's owner is an Italian artist who divides his time between Europe and Brazil, and while off the island he leaves several of his works half-finished on easels throughout the hotel. Such is the pace of the Marco Polo.

Time seems to stand still here, and our days were long in the best sense of the word—long leisurely meals, long naps, long conversations in the courtyard. The singular pace of life here is what makes the house an oasis, a cheerful, romantic shrine in the midst of a thriving island town. Finding the right accommodation can transform how guests experience a place, and, as I learned, the trick to Rhodes is to move beyond those hectic main streets. The Marco Polo is precisely the right place to explore the hidden secrets of this ancient island city—and to spend time doing nothing at all.

DON'T MISS

Sculptures, mosaics, and figurines at the Archaeological Museum of Rhodes; impossibly fresh seafood at Nireas, for lunch or dinner; the medieval splendor of the Palace of the Grand Master; a jaunt over to Lindos on the east side of the island, where the ruins are best experienced at sunset. We also took an unforgettable day trip to the nearby island of Symi, which is known for its isolated beaches, funky pastel-colored houses, and lively port; visit Symi in late summer and dance with the locals all night long as traditional musicians play in the town square.

At the Marco Polo, there are unfinished paintings lying around, and you feel like you're living in a mysterious artist's atelier.

Color is everywhere you look. Very few can mix all these shades in just seven rooms and get away with it.

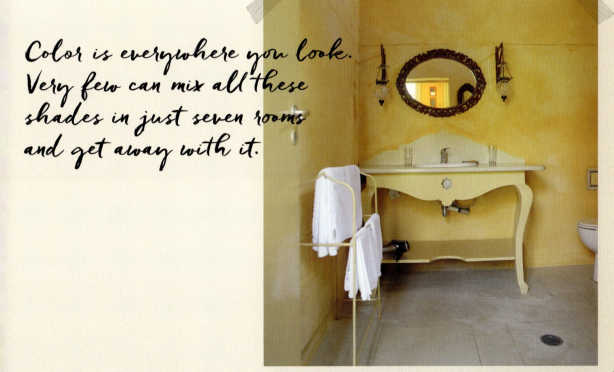

Efi manages the day-to-day operations at the Marco Polo Mansion. She was like our mother, providing tips on where to go and how to get there and even personally picking us up at the port when we arrived.

OLD MARKETS, SYMI

Too many museums and medieval forts can make kids a bit anxious—a quick escape to Symi is perfect for a couple of days on its idyllic beaches.

There isn't any shopping at Symi's Old Markets—not anymore, at least. The building used to be an ancient marketplace for sponges and silver and has been converted into a five-room hotel. A short ferry ride away from Rhodes, the island of Symi is the perfect size to conquer with an overnight trip—and the colorful, elegant rooms at the Old Markets are the ideal place to rest.

Elegant and delicious, The Muses is the caliber of restaurant you would never expect to find on the tiny island of Symi, and it's owned by Argentinians! Try the sashimi with strawberries and ginger foam—sublime.

Make sure to stop by the rooftop terrace at the Old Markets— great cocktails and even greater views.

UWAJIMA, SHIKOKU, JAPAN
KIYA RYOKAN

THE DISCOVERY

"Journey to a far-off part of Japan, beyond the farthest reaches of tourism, where the culture and hospitality are as real and peaceful as the sound of gentle waves lapping on its rocky shores."

THE DESTINATION

Mountains run east to west across Shikoku, the smallest of Japan's four major islands, and most residents live on the northern shore facing inland toward Hiroshima and Osaka. South of the mountains is an unspoiled paradise of deciduous forests and rocky coastlines. The climate is a little warmer here than in the rest of Japan, making it an ideal place to grow citrus fruits, including oranges, yuzu, and mikan. On the western shore of Shikoku is Uwajima, a serene coastal town that looks out across the deep blue waters of the Uwa Sea.

Kiya Ryokan is the place to stay in this distant part of the world. Founded in 1911, it is a two-story wooden house built in the traditional style of the nineteenth-century Meiji period—a shining example of the quiet, zen-filled mood that permeates Shikoku's tranquil shores. Sliding doors, tatami mats, and transparent paper walls contribute to its permanently hushed ambience, and there is more breathing room and space to move around here than would ever be found in any of Japan's urban *ryokan*. This place creates such a magically refined environment with so little—so it came as no surprise when I learned that this part of Japan is famous for its haiku poets.

DON'T MISS

For such a small town, Uwajima has many things to see, and anyone at the Kiya Ryokan will be happy to provide further directions. Start by checking out the small shop inside the inn, with a selection of local delicacies and artisanal products. Consider a private dinner at Ikadaya, twenty minutes north of town, where delicious seafood is served aboard a raft and only one group can dine at a time; an afternoon trip to Doi Pearl Farm, the only pearl harvesting operation that offers up-close tours of this ancient Japanese practice; a visit to the Dairaku-ji temple, which is inhabited by the most adorable flying squirrels that glide every night from the top of the temple to the ground to nibble on fallen maple and cherry tree leaves; and a drive up and down the coast, with striking views of terraced fields that fall gracefully into the sea.

Nothing beats the perfect symmetry of a tatami room.

HARBOUR ISLAND, BAHAMAS

OCEAN VIEW CLUB

THE DISCOVERY

"Anyone who has stayed at the Ocean View Club on Harbour Island knows that it's never called the Ocean View Club—it's called "Pip's" after the incredible matriarch of the house, who recently passed on her Bahamian word-of-mouth lodge to her son Ben. Having lived her early life in Europe as a trained Le Cordon Bleu chef before moving to this secluded island, Pip is a tour de force of a woman. Sarcastic, opinionated, and brazen in the best way, she would walk from room to room with a cigarette on her lips and would never hesitate to speak her mind. Newcomers might now meet her by chance when she stops by to visit her son and old guests who are like family to her.

I remember the first time I went to Harbour Island. Pip and I were on her terrace, enjoying a lunch of fresh fish as we discussed life and relationships and shared a healthy dose of gossip. All of a sudden, she looked at me, took the cigarette out of her mouth, and asked, "Do you know Alexandre de Betak?" I nearly fell out of my seat: Alex and I had met a month prior in Buenos Aires and were just flirting, but there was no way that Pip could possibly have known that—right? Alex had been vacationing at Pip's for years, and although Pip had known me for only a day or two, she could sense that he and I could be a good match."

ABOVE: The one and only Pip, one of the most famous people in the fashion industry.

Chess is more fun when the pieces are giant!

THE DESTINATION

Harbour Island's unforgettable pink sands have captured creative minds for decades, and many photographers and other fashion folk have found inspiration at Pip's while doing their shoots. It all began when Francis Giacobetti and Bruce Weber discovered the place in the late seventies; then came Gilles Bensimon, Anna Wintour, Naomi Campbell, Jean-Baptiste Mondino, and Cindy Crawford. But the best part is that Pip keeps souvenir photos from these shoots in frames all over the walls of her house—so although the decor is somewhat on the rustic yet colorful side, there are hints of understated glamour in every niche.

Still, the most compelling part of Pip's, now Ben's, is the family at the center of it all, and the house itself is a natural extension of their sensibilities. Whereas so many places in the Caribbean are overcleaned, overglossed, overdecorated resorts, the Ocean View Club still feels like a home. I love to stay in one of the quiet cottages tucked a short walk away from the main house—the ones that used to be the rooms of Pip and her sons.

DON'T MISS

Scuba diving, paddleboarding, and bone fishing, or just relaxing on the pink sand beaches; driving golf carts around the pastel-colored island and stopping by Pip's vintage shop, Miss Mae; getting conch salad at Angela's Starfish Restaurant; bareback galloping along the beach on the most beautiful horses; playing a life-size game of chess on Ocean View's terrace; and going into the port town at night to party with the locals.

OPPOSITE, BOTTOM LEFT: After working up an appetite, take complete advantage of Pip's Le Cordon Bleu–trained staff—every meal is freshly caught or harvested that morning, including lemongrass curry lobster for dinner and mounds of succulent fruit for dessert. Pip didn't believe in writing out menus, so you were at the mercy of her surprises. Nowadays, Charlie, Ben's wife, has updated their ways and created a short list with their classic dishes, though you can still ask Ben to surprise you with his delicious cocktails, his most famous being a killer frozen margarita.

I couldn't resist going for a canter on the beach and taking my beautiful horse for a little bath in the open sea!

Don't forget to rent a golf cart and explore the island.
There are incredible sights to be enjoyed next to the old marina!

MÉRIDA, MEXICO
HACIENDA SANTA ROSA

THE DISCOVERY

"I have always had a great affinity with Mexicans. I guess it's the Latin ease and joyous energy that attracts me to them. So when a friend invited me to the Yucatán Peninsula to visit a few haciendas, I signed up without hesitation."

THE DESTINATION

The road south from Mérida's airport traverses thick jungles before reaching Maxcanú, where the trees start to thin and the road leads to a village of small colorful churches and thatched-roof homes. At the end of the village sits Hacienda Santa Rosa, a former nobleman's estate from the nineteenth century. A veranda anchored by graceful arches overlooks a large lawn, and the walkway leading up to the house is framed by palm trees. Each of the eleven guest rooms is unique, well proportioned, and private, with hand-carved wood furniture, cool polished tile floors, and gauzy canopies over the bed. My room had a private plunge pool, hidden under the shade of mahogany trees and magenta-hued bougainvillea vines, where I could soak away the afternoon to the sound of cicadas buzzing and the ethereal smell of some sweet unknown flower floating on the breeze.

"Not far from the main house, there are several different workshops with twenty or so women who specialize in local techniques such as embroidery, metalwork, and filigree. These descendants of the ancient Maya have revived centuries-old handicraft techniques thanks to Carola, the wife of the hacienda's manager, and her nonprofit organization that has served the area for over ten years, empowering the local communities by creating spaces for them to develop their skills and finding new markets for their artistry. The goal of this trip was for us to work with these women and help them develop different lines of products, but after a few days of braiding baskets, hammering silver, cross-stitching linen handkerchiefs, and engaging with them, it became clear that they had much more to teach us than the other way around.

The Luxury Collection has renovated this colonial mansion, maintaining every original detail.

 At the end of our trip, our group celebrated with a big Yucatán-style dinner. Seated on the Santa Rosa's elegant veranda, we started at dusk as golden light streamed through the palm trees and fell onto the hacienda's elegant front columns. We indulged in *sopa de lima*, chili-spiced beef, and probably a bit too much mezcal—when in Mexico, right?

 As dinner began to wind down, everyone seemed tired and ready for sleep. I was, too, but then I heard the festive sounds of *cumbia* coming from the darkness beyond the hacienda's gate. My curiosity was piqued (or maybe it was the tequila), so I rallied a group to see what was going on. The music got louder as we approached, the drumbeats more booming; then we emerged from the woods to find ourselves in the middle of a huge fiesta being held by the townspeople. We ended up dancing all night long with the locals and the band, and it wasn't until the morning sun began to creep over the horizon that we headed back to the hacienda, exhausted, breathless, and euphoric from our unexpected night out.

DON'T MISS

Staring up in wonder beneath the ancient pyramids at Uxmal, where it feels like the earth itself exhales power; learning to make *cochinita pibil*—slow-roasted pork with traditional spices and sour orange—in a cooking class lead by locals; diving in sacred Mayan cenote caves; and my best advice: If you hear music coming from beyond the hacienda's walls, don't be afraid to find out where it's coming from.

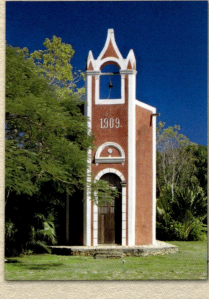

TOP: The swimming pool was once a well that captured and stored rainwater.
CENTER LEFT: The manager's wife, Carola Diez, empowers local women by helping them develop their crafts to sell in the marketplace.

MAKGADIKGADI PAN, BOTSWANA
JACK'S CAMP

THE DISCOVERY

"Considering its harsh and desolate location, Jack's Camp is something of a mirage. First, visitors fly to Johannesburg, then on to Maun, Botswana. From there, it's necessary to charter a small propeller plane over the Kalahari Desert to the heart of Botswana's wild savannah, and it is here that the dozen or so large tents of Jack's Camp are found, each built from drab, sturdy-looking canvas. There is nothing around but untamed wilderness for hundreds of miles. Approaching the camp, it does not look like much, but pull back the front flap of a tent to discover a decadent oasis of luxury: the walls lined with rich maroon jacquards, the polished mahogany floors strewn with Persian rugs, and the furniture elegantly hand-fashioned from local woods. There are many places to go on safari in Africa, but only Jack's Camp transports travelers back to the golden age of exploration, when only the brave ventured to these far-off lands in search of adventure—and one never knew what might be encountered in the bush."

Despite the extravagant decor, you can always feel the beauty of immaculate nature in Africa.

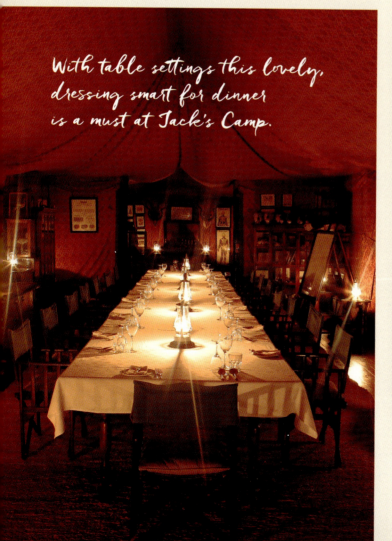

With table settings this lovely, dressing smart for dinner is a must at Jack's Camp.

The camp's library and collection of artifacts designate it as a national museum of Botswana.

THE DESTINATION

The Makgadikgadi Pan, where Jack's Camp is located, is an expansive salt flat, situated in the center of Botswana's arid savannah, which is one of the largest of its kind in the world. Geologists agree that this land was once an enormous lake, having dried up thousands of years ago, leaving only salt rocks and low-lying grasses in its place. Today, during the dry season, the Makgadikgadi Pan becomes a harsh environment—almost nothing can survive its hot, barren, lunar landscape. But once the rains come, it blooms into life with a rich population of meerkats, wildebeest, flamingos, zebras, lizards, lions, and ostriches, making it an excellent place to go on safari and experience nature's most elemental form.

The camp's namesake, Jack Bousfield, was a mid-twentieth-century trapper and explorer who traveled all over Africa before setting up his camp on the edge of the Makgadikgadi Pan, where he lived until his death in 1992. His son Ralph renovated the camp and now hosts guests there throughout the year, inviting only the bravest travelers to come experience this rugged outpost. The place serves as his homage to traditional 1940s safari style—each tent is decorated with old books, candles ensconced in hurricane lamps, and black-and-white photographs of famous explorers—and if Ralph happens to be at the camp, visitors can see what an incredible safari expert he is. Having grown up on the camp alongside the bushmen, Ralph has come face-to-face with wild leopards and experienced unimaginable danger in the wild. But don't take my word for it—come nightfall, gather round the campfire and listen as Ralph recounts one of his many escapades.

DON'T MISS

Safari, safari, safari! Keep an eye out for meerkats trying to sneak into tents in search of a snack. Enjoy a surprisingly elegant tea service before heading out in the bush for adventure, because even in the bush, Jack's Camp likes to maintain a degree of civility; speed along on ATVs as fast as riders can handle—there are no speed limits in this part of the world; visit unspoiled archaeological sites to see fossil beds of extinct giant zebras and hippopotamus; swim in the camp's pool, which sits in the middle of a gorgeous wooden deck; and best of all, enjoy long dinners under the stars, spent sharing exploration stories with fellow campers.

I highly recommend walking safaris wearing a silk dress!

ENTRE RÍOS, ARGENTINA
LOS OMBUES LODGE

THE DISCOVERY

"My father has always been quite a character. A tall, handsome man, he is the kind of dad who comes alive when he has an audience—he loves to sit at the head of a dinner table, wave his arms, and tell long, epic stories in his booming voice. My two sisters and I inherited his strong, inky, perceptive eyes, and at each of our weddings, he walked us down the aisle like it was his moment to shine, not the bride's— but his pride makes us love him all the more. Now that he owns and operates his own hunting lodge north of Buenos Aires, every time I visit I get to share in the immense happiness it brings him to be the king of his castle, at one with nature in this bucolic stretch of Argentina."

THE DESTINATION

The province of Entre Ríos sits, as its name suggests, between the Paraná and Uruguay rivers just a few hours' drive north of Buenos Aires. The fertile farmlands and gently rolling pampas here are idyllic, much more accessible and less untamed than the wilds of Patagonia. My father has been leading expeditions through this area for as long as I can remember, and when I was a young girl of maybe six or seven, he had the opportunity to build a lodge of his own, which he called Los Ombues, after the iconic, stocky evergreen trees that grow on his 42,000-acre property.

Today, my father's lodge is one of the best bird hunting sites anywhere, and I'm not saying that just because he is my dad! He maintains over three hundred acres of sunflower, corn, wheat, and soy crops on the property, making this one of the best roosting grounds for dove hunting—and it goes without saying that it is also one of the most gorgeous tracts of land around when all those golden sunflowers bloom in the summer. Los Ombues is also known to avid hunters like Jack Nicklaus, Tom Watson, and even Prince Harry as being well worth the long flight south to Argentina, as it is one of the few places in the world where travelers can hunt duck, partridge, and dove all on the same property.

While others see doves to hunt, I see a beautiful sunset.

My sisters and I were never really into hunting, and my poor father would have loved a son to take on these trips—but now he has his sons-in-law!

Family reunion at Los Ombues— three generations and three husbands.

But for my sisters and me—who, for better or for worse, never really took to hunting—the lodge is filled with memories: Not only did we assist with the planting of trees, laying of bricks, and troweling of mortar when it was built, but our childhood paintings decorate the walls and the rooms are filled with objects brought home from our travels. For us, the house is a nostalgic patchwork of memories: We first learned to drive in the fields here; we built tree houses up in the big Ombues; Delia, who took care of the house before she passed away, was like a grandmother to all of us; and we spent countless nights giggling over board games well past our bedtimes.

As someone who travels so much, I find the best part of coming to Los Ombues is not simply that it feels like home, but rather getting to see behind the scenes and witness the immeasurable joy it brings my father to play host. Having grown up here, where all sorts of travelers would pass through our estancia, I was exposed to their different outlooks and cultures. As a practical matter, interacting with these people was how I learned to speak English. But on a deeper level, it also profoundly shaped both my *desire* to travel and the *way* I travel. From a young age, I saw the value of vacationing to a place like my father's lodge. Because for a short time, guests aren't staying in an impersonal hotel or chain resort—they are staying in my father's home, where he welcomes all with open arms to experience his way of life in this tiny slice of paradise.

DON'T MISS

Big, hearty dinners of exceptional meats caught fresh that day, paired with plenty of Argentinian Malbec; riding horseback through glittering waters of vast shallow marshland and spotting thousands of feeding cattle; flying in from Buenos Aires on my dad's plane, which he lands directly on the property; having a glass of wine by the lawn and enjoying the stars at night; and hanging on every word as my father shares his most treasured hunting stories.

TRANCOSO, BRAZIL

UXUA

THE DISCOVERY

"In the state of Bahia, Brazil, there is a secluded stretch of coast where the rainforest gradually thins out and dissolves successively into palm trees, then brush, then immaculate white sand beaches. This is Trancoso, a pristine beach town quietly, unassumingly overlooking the South Atlantic. This distant hideaway attracts people from all over looking to disconnect with the world and reconnect with themselves. At the center of it all is the quadrado, *a town square and UNESCO World Heritage site around which are scattered a handful of colorful houses, restaurants, and shops. Surreal wild horses trot out of the woods before lying down to rest in the grass, and monkeys swing through the trees overhead. It is a mystical place, where bohemian luxury meets unspoiled nature like nowhere else I have seen. Time stands still in Trancoso, and magic floats on the air like a warm breeze."*

THE DESTINATION

At the head of the *quadrado* stands the São João Batista Church, a spotless white building perched amid the village's lush vegetation and vivid colors. The church dates to Trancoso's colonization in 1585, though people have been living here for much longer. There is a colorful and vibrant history here, and the inhabitants have a contagious sense of joyfulness—I could tell from their smiles that they constantly enjoy life.

I made the journey with my sister and her husband not long after the birth of their son, the first baby boy in the family; Trancoso, although remote, was the perfect place for us to share some time together in rustic luxury. We stayed at Uxua (*oo-SHOO-ahh*), a series of houses and structures hidden between the *quadrado* and the local fishermen's homes. Some of the property's casas date back five hundred years, and all of them have been meticulously refurbished by the owner, visionary Dutch designer Wilbert Das. He has such a love for details and manages to find the perfect balance between authenticity,

Because of the handmade furniture and bohemian design, each room at Uxua has its own personality and character.

style, and comfort. No two rooms are alike, as each is outfitted with handmade furniture and original pieces of art. Wilbert employed local artisans and craftsmen for everything, from the lamp on each night table to the night table itself, which were all made using typical local techniques. That, I found, is the charm of Uxua—its aesthetic is directly drawn from the creative culture of the people who live there, so it feels like a seamless part of this enchanting beach village.

Each morning I would open my casa doors and walk directly onto the *quadrado* to start the day with impossibly succulent tropical fruits and tapioca pancakes. After a slow breakfast—nobody rushes in Trancoso—I would spend more time wandering barefoot through town to explore artisan shops before heading down to the *praia* for a swim and a drink at the Uxua beach bar. Wilbert lives on-site at Uxua, which makes guests staying there feel like they are truly in someone's home. He opens his doors to every single guest by sharing his life, offering advice on everything from where to eat and play to the best hidden spots along the beach to have some time alone. Uxua is his vision of organic luxury come to life, and discovering Trancoso with his guidance makes this place feel all the more extraordinary, like an imaginary tropical paradise that is somehow strangely familiar.

DON'T MISS

A bike ride through the nearby Buffalo Valley—the area is known for excellent birdwatching, and, as its name suggests, large herds of buffalo; cooling off at the beach with a lunch of fresh ceviche and coconut water straight from the fruit; lapping up an açai after playing some volleyball or Frisbee; and visiting all the local artisans in town for art, objets, and locally sourced coconut oil beauty products to bring home. And as magical as Trancoso is during the day under the hot Brazilian sun, make sure to spend some time visiting the local bars at night to listen to traditional live music and linger over a caipirinha, watching locals dance *forró*.

Your private bar on Uxua's beach is the best place to enjoy cocktails at sunset.

Dragon fruit, passion fruit, mango.... Nothing compares to the fruit selection here.

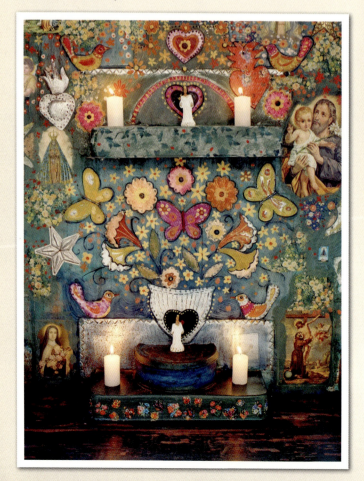

White party! In Brazil, there is always reason to celebrate.

MALLORCA, SPAIN
SA PALOSA

THE DISCOVERY

"Mallorca is a huge island with many different pockets, some more hidden than others, so one person's Mallorca can be very different from another's. There are party towns, sleepy hippie enclaves, remote beaches, tourist beaches, tranquil fields, and romantic hideaways. Personally, I hold a special place in my heart for the secluded north side of the island where we spend our summers. Alex's oldest friends, the first to host him there, are Chaime and Jorge, a bohemian Spanish couple who have been on the island for over twenty-five years. Seeing Mallorca through their eyes is always a deeply relaxing, gratifying experience. Getting to their place is no easy feat, however, because they live in the last house all the way at the top of a road that snakes its way up a steep mountain— a road that, at its narrowest point, can barely accommodate the smallest of cars. But once travelers finally make it to the top, they are greeted by a view of hills covered in countless olive trees rolling off into the distance, the natural energy of sunshine bouncing off the rocks, and—best of all—the unconditionally warm smiles of the most extraordinary hosts."

THE DESTINATION

Sóller is an ancient port on Mallorca's northern shore, and the town's focal point is Saint Bartholomew Church. The structure dates back to the thirteenth century, and its peaceful plaza gets completely taken over at the end of every August, when the Esclatabutzes group celebrates the town's patron with a pyrotechnics show that has been going on for centuries. The members of this group dress up as demons and throw fireworks all around while all of us dance to the rhythm of their drums, wearing long-sleeved hoodies that we have to soak every five minutes in the water fountain to avoid getting burnt! The party always ends at the Plaza del Mercado, where the firemen throw their water on the crowd, and where bouncing beds and inflatable castles are set up so we can all become kids again.

Chaime and Jorge—always cooking, always smiling!

Chaime and Jorge split their time between Madrid, where they have an organic vegetarian restaurant called Sopa; Bali, where they run a jewelry business; and Mallorca, where they have become the ultimate hosts for an enchanting and relaxing retreat. Throughout the years, they have bought up a handful of little stone-facade casitas atop one of the more out-of-the-way mountains, refurbished them, and now invite guests to stay and experience this little slice of rustic tranquility. Today, their life is a comfortable routine of entertaining, meditating, jewelry designing, cooking fabulously delicious and rich vegetarian foods, and taking care of the friendly donkey they have as a pet.

Chaime and Jorge live to take care of their loved ones, and their optimistic outlook is infectious. I remember once there was a big storm on the island—overnight, the skies started to hail chunks of ice the size of plums, breaking many windows in the area and making many residents furious. When we woke up the following morning, our hosts' motorbike had slid about ten meters away from where they had parked it the night before, smashed and practically totaled. But instead of complaining, Chaime and Jorge found it extremely funny and could not stop laughing about "the odyssey of the bike."

DON'T MISS

Snacking on as many *gambas de Sóller* as you can handle at Cala Deià; renting a boat in the port of Sóller and sailing to Sa Foradada for a gigantic paella and diving in crystal water caves on the way back; riding a Vespa up and down the craggy mountain roads; visiting Consell Market on Sunday mornings to get handmade ceramics at Pere Coll's; going to Ca Na Toneta for dinner; and, of course, long nights filled with wine and storytelling, spent with Chaime and Jorge.

ABOVE: No trip to Mallorca's northern shore is complete without trying the paella at Sa Foradada.
OPPOSITE, CLOCKWISE FROM TOP LEFT: After a long and delicious lunch, enjoy the sunset in S'Estaca, a coastal fishing hamlet where sixteen small cottages nestle in the rocks; every August, we celebrate the patron of Sóller, Saint Bartholomew, with a fire party.

GARZÓN, URUGUAY
CASA ANNA

THE DISCOVERY

"The two-hour drive from Montevideo out to José Ignacio has become a well-worn path, as the seaside town is now a popular destination for weekenders and visitors from all over the world. I love visiting its beaches, but the town itself has become just a bit too popular for my taste— traffic and long waits at restaurants are not my recipe for summer holidays. Luckily, there are a few escapes for the less social. Just half an hour or so beyond the crowds of José Ignacio, hidden on arid plains and rocky sierras, is an oasis of refinement, luxurious in its isolation: Pueblo Garzón."

THE DESTINATION

For a long time, there wasn't much to Garzón. Originally a railroad stop between Montevideo and Rocha, the town grew during the 1920s but was eventually abandoned once train travel was replaced by car travel. It was essentially a ghost town until chef Francis Mallmann, always a pioneer and visionary, fell in love with its rural elegance and opened a restaurant and two-room inn there called the Hotel Garzón. A handful of other restaurateurs have set their sights on Garzón, but the town has largely retained its remote, peaceful character.

London-based art dealer Martin Summers and his wife, Annie, are two of the growing number of people who have fallen for the allure and grace of this distant outpost. In 2006, they decided to buy a few acres here and build a home where they could escape the London winters for a few months a year. When Martin and Annie are not present, they open their home to guests—there are six casitas that can be rented out individually or as a whole unit—so anyone willing to make the journey can experience the profound tranquility of this far-off slice of paradise. Not a single detail is overlooked in any of the rooms, and all of them open onto the property's extensive gardens, lined with agapanthus and surrounding a gorgeous swimming pool.

My first impression of Garzón was that
I had arrived in a ghost town from the Wild West.

Chilling out, reading, lying by the pool.... There is a simple charm in having nothing to do.

DON'T MISS

Luckily, José Ignacio is only a half hour's drive away, so visitors can enjoy the stunning beaches and dining in town all day, then retreat to the solitude of Garzón at night. Make sure to try the dulce de leche volcanoes at La Huella, and an afternoon of drinks at La Caracola, located on the beach but accessible only by boat; if heading to La Barra, enjoy a dozen Medialunas Calentitas, the best croissants ever; and make sure to return to Garzón at night. Try the tangy cucumber gazpacho and grilled prawns at Lucifer, a six-table restaurant founded by Mallmann's protégée Lucia Soria, then return to Casa Anna after dinner—at night, the hosts set up a screen by the pool and play vintage gaucho movies under the stars.

OPPOSITE, CENTER RIGHT: Martin at one of his parties with my mother, Maita, and stepdad, Buby.

POSITANO, ITALY
VILLA TREVILLE

THE DISCOVERY

"Alex and I arrived in Positano in the middle of the night in a dreamlike haze, having just landed in Naples and driven the ninety-minute journey through darkness along the meandering, mountainous Amalfi Coast. We knew very little about Villa TreVille before our arrival there—it was referred to us by friends— and the moment we were shown to our private villa, we fell asleep. But the next morning, a warm Tyrrhenian sunshine carefully crept in through our windows and the view outside came to life: white fishermen's boats gliding across azure waters picking up the morning's catch; immense rocky cliffs tumbling into the heart of the sea; dotted clusters of canary, blush pink, and pale blue houses; and a vast, glittering sea stretching out as far as imagination could reach."

THE DESTINATION

The allure of Positano is that just by visiting this iconic place, one might feel like an Italian movie star; and the allure of Villa TreVille is that it was once the home of none other than the maestro Franco Zeffirelli. The film and opera director discovered Positano while on a bike tour in 1941, when it was a sleepy port town accessible only by boat or by a mule path through the mountains—before it was a tourist destination and before countless authors, filmmakers, or musicians were seduced by its magic.

Positano's magical vistas inspire all who travel there.

Cinematic views await around every corner of Villa TreVille.

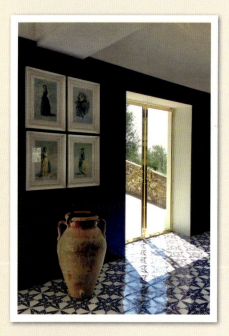

Zeffirelli returned years later to build Villa TreVille here, and today every inch of the property exudes the nostalgia of his influence. Each of the villas is named after a different member of the artistic entourage he brought with him to Positano: Leonard Bernstein, Sergei Diaghilev, and Richard Dowes, among others. The rooms are decadently spacious—a feature travelers might not get if they stay directly in the somewhat cramped Positano town—and tastefully appointed with more than enough chaises and daybeds on which to soak up some sun. A deliciously warm breeze flows from room to room, carrying the seductive aromas of salty ocean air and fresh lemons.

Just knowing which artistic legends have passed through TreVille's elegant halls lends the place a sense of timeless glamour; its historic guests notwithstanding, this place is also unique by virtue of its position and character. The property itself sits on a cliff overlooking Positano, a modest distance away from the town but reachable by a quick boat or Vespa ride, meaning that it allows all its guests to choose whether they seek to rest in TreVille's solitude or take advantage of Positano's *dolce vita*. And the property is perched several hundred feet below the access road, so there is no traffic or hustle and bustle— only the sea, the sun, and those who seek respite in this fabulously luxurious hideaway.

DON'T MISS

A leisurely Vespa ride up and down the winding roads around Amalfi, no destination necessary; going to the beach in Positano to see all the colorful umbrellas, or staying at TreVille's private beach for some alone time; climbing up and over the Walk of the Gods to the nearby town of Praiano, then jumping off the rocks and into the sea; sailing to Lo Scoglio da Tommaso in Nerano for a zucchini pasta that will induce sleep for hours; visiting the Amatruda paper mill in Amalfi to buy their delicate deckle-edge paper; going to Le Sirenuse for cocktails at sunset and stopping by their boutique, Carla's Emporio.

Le Sirenuse's boutique, Carla's Emporio, is a must for printed shirts, caftans, and hats.

Rent a boat and go to Nerano for some delicious zucchini pasta!

OPPOSITE, BOTTOM: The most exquisite paper mill, Amatruda, is located just half an hour away, and I rode there one afternoon on a scooter I had rented in search of paper for my wedding invitations. I showed up and asked to meet the owner, and he graciously gave me an after-hours tour of the whole factory.

MENDOZA, ARGENTINA
FINCA LOS ALAMOS

THE DISCOVERY

"As a place I have often visited with my cousins and grandparents for family reunions, Los Alamos is special to me. I have always felt a deep admiration for Susana Bombal, a writer, world traveler, and all-around avant-garde woman who owned this finca as her country home from the 1930s to the 1960s. She surrounded herself with the most interesting and fascinating people of her time, including writers Richard Llewellyn, Manuel Mujica Láinez, and Jorge Luis Borges, with whom she shared a profound friendship. She traveled the world and brought pieces back to decorate Los Alamos—jacquards from Paris, wallpapers from Florence, armchairs from England, and sculptures from Seville. A patron of the arts, Bombal also lined the walls with paintings by her friends Raúl Soldi, Héctor Basaldúa, and Norah Borges. Having no children, she passed the property down to her nephews Camilo and César Aldao Bombal, who have preserved it, all the while making sure that Susana's free, creative spirit can still be felt in every corner."

THE DESTINATION

Ruta Nacional 7 stretches out from the west side of Buenos Aires, where it rolls across the open pampas and then ascends upward through snowcapped mountains on its way to Santiago, Chile. Here, in the foothills of the Andes, lies Mendoza, the heart of South America's winemaking culture and a crossroads for adventurous passersby. In its heyday, Finca Los Alamos was originally a half-million-acre ranch, focused on cattle farming and anchored by its grand old manor dating back to 1830. Today, the estate is around 12,000 acres, and most of the irrigated land is given over to extensive vineyards, olive orchards, garlic groves, sweet pepper plots, and orangeries.

At Los Alamos, you can commission your own barrel of wine, made precisely to your specifications. My father got one for me and each of my sisters on our wedding days.

Los Alamos is a pioneering vineyard in the region, with much of the production focusing on Malbec, a variety of grape that thrives in the high altitude. In the autumn, those vines turn an alluring shade of crimson; some of my favorite memories include horseback riding through rows upon rows of these vines after the harvest, where, at twilight, the sun scatters warm rose-hued light through the land, making for a breathtaking spectacle almost too picturesque to be real.

The red adobe colonial manor itself is most characterful, with traces of the finca's intriguing history everywhere—originally a frontier fort surrounded by a moat to protect from roving Indians, it is replaced today by solemn poplar groves. Bedrooms open onto an enclosed courtyard where flowering bushes grow, and there is a swimming pool and a great poplar tree filled with cooing pigeons, beneath which sit wrought iron chairs. The time-worn wooden floors are inlaid with rare orange tree woods that grow on the finca, and the ceilings are made from rough-hewn plaster beams handmade by local Araucanian tribesmen.

My favorite room has a pink full wall mural, painted by Héctor Basaldúa, depicting a carnival parade. The dining room is full of charm with its gray stone floor, thick adobe walls, fireplace with two cherub wood carvings sitting on the mantel, cordovan chairs, and an antique brass scale transformed into a chandelier—it's a cozy decor with a patina that pairs well with exquisite dinners of homemade *ñoquis*, or of empanadas cooked in the traditional mud oven and *asados* served in the shade of the poplar trees with the sound of the glistening water. After a long day of roaming the grounds, nothing beats curling up by the big stone fireplace with a stack of antique books and magazines pilfered from the finca's remarkable library.

A highlight of the estate is the Borgesian Labyrinth, dreamed and designed by Randoll Coate, an English diplomat and friend of Susana and Borges, and the legacy of Camilo Aldao, Jr., who made it come true: In Aldao's words, "built to be seen from the sky, only visible to the eyes of an eagle or angel"—someone like himself. Inspired by Borges's labyrinthine stories and *The Garden of Forking Paths*, the Borgesian Labyrinth takes the shape of an open book with Borges's name reflected in a mirror, with Borgesian symbols like the hourglass, his walking cane, the year '86 since he died at 86 in 1986, and so on. I love getting lost in the romance and nostalgia of the maze. About Susana, Borges wrote, "She is where music is, and in the gentle blue of the sky, in Greek hexameters. And in our solitude, which seeks her out."

DON'T MISS

Getting lost in the Borges Labyrinth and climbing up the watchtower to enjoy the views; winery hopping to taste the region's best offerings straight out of the barrel; starting by the Bombal y Aldao winery and visiting the thriving olive oil plantations; a sunrise ride in the Andes or a pack trip across the cordillera to Chile; white-water rafting through a rimrock canyon in the Andean foothills; wandering the country lanes lined with wildflowers and forty-foot poplars; trout fishing in the streams that wind through the finca's sister estate; an evening barbecue at the ranch where local townspeople are invited over for folk music and dancing; spelunking nearby caves with ancient indigenous paintings; shopping for authentic gaucho clothes and horse tack in the nearby town of San Rafael; and, of course, drinking more than your fill of the region's excellent wines.

A huge labyrinth in homage to Argentinian writer Jorge Luis Borges, who was a regular at the finca.

My first time at Los Alamos was on a family trip we took with our grandparents and cousins!

ABOVE, TOP: Many artists stay at Los Alamos and leave their mark there, including Héctor Basaldúa, who painted this wall.

PATMOS, GREECE
ARCHONTARIKI

THE DISCOVERY

"Alex and I travel constantly, always packing our bags, driving to the airport, boarding planes, deboarding planes, driving back from the airport.... So for one of our first big holidays together, we were completely smitten with the idea of chartering a boat; after all, during a sailing trip, the boat becomes home, and it's easy to explore many different places without having to constantly pack and unpack. We set our sights on the Aegean, where nothing could be more romantic than sailing one of those traditional wooden gulets from island to island, spending a night or two on each, just a couple of adventurers on the open sea. We had originally planned on spending only one night on Patmos, but once we docked in its main town of Skala, we were absolutely enchanted and decided to extend our stay. The fresh and salty ocean air, the purity of the white architecture, the almost magical feeling of standing where Greeks had stood for thousands of years.... We had much more to experience on Patmos than one night could possibly allow."

THE DESTINATION

People who visit Patmos often talk about its mystical energy. Not only has the island been inhabited by Greeks for as long as humanity can remember, but it is also where John the Apostle wrote the Book of Revelation. There is no airport on Patmos, making for a much smaller flow of people and near absence of tourism, and it doesn't hurt that there are no nightclubs or rowdy bars as there are on so many other islands—here there are only a handful of tavernas open late for drinks.

Many of the homes on Patmos are surrounded by windowless walls, so you never know what mysteries wait on the other side....

Publicist Karla Otto, a regular on Patmos, had been urging us for years to visit and was able to refer me to a secret little guesthouse in the town of Chora, located up in the hills away from the port of Skala. I have never been able to decide if I believe in superstition or not, but there was something about walking through that ancient town that I can't explain. Impeccably preserved, the streets are narrow, and many of the houses have courtyard walls with no windows—so wherever travelers walk, they feel as if, on the other side of any given door, a hidden world is waiting to be found. Wherever we went on the island, from caves to beaches to meandering alleyways, my thirst for discovery only continued to grow.

Our rooms at the Archontariki were refined and neutral, decorated with local woods and lots of Greek whites and blues. We would explore all day, come back for a restful night's sleep, have a quick breakfast in the morning, and then take off on the scooter we rented and do it all over again the next day.

Annie, our beautiful host.

DON'T MISS

Octopus: every type, in every single way! I have never had so much octopus as I did here. At each restaurant, make sure to ask servers all about how the dish was prepared—every chef has their own technique. My favorite was at Pantheon, a restaurant just inside the entrance to Chora. Renting a scooter is the best way to see Patmos: Spend an afternoon zipping around the Byzantine fortress surrounding the Monastery of St. John; park at Petra and take a dive in the mystical waters believed to have once been a site for worship of the goddess Aphrodite; stop at Niko's, a trailer on the road with the best view on the island; and round off the night with drinks by the water at any of the tavernas by the port in Skala.

In Patmos, you can have octopus for every meal,
and no two places prepare it the same.
We had it with olive oil, with spices, with
red wine, with white wine, braised, grilled....

Just outside town, you'll find the charming chiringuito Nikko's, a food truck of sorts with the best snacks and views of the beach.

LAIKIPIA, KENYA
OL MALO

THE DISCOVERY

"Several years back, while traveling through South Africa, I was about to fly up to visit a boyfriend in Kenya and, unfortunately, we broke up just days before my departure. I decided to move forward with the Kenya trip anyway—the plane was booked, and I was not about to change my plans because of a man! This, however, meant finding a new place to stay on very short notice. Luckily, my mother was able to connect me with the Francombe family, fourth-generation Kenyans and the owners of a safari lodge called Ol Malo.

Being newly single, traveling on my own, and having never been to Kenya, I had no idea what to expect. But the moment my plane touched down in the vast savannah, I felt a connection to this place. There was a pulse to being in such a remote part of the world and an excitement in knowing that I was about to embark on a rare adventure. And, as I was about to learn, there is nothing more incredible than the remote, the unique, and the unknown."

THE DESTINATION

Many tourists to this part of the world visit the Maasai Mara National Reserve, which is one of Africa's leading destinations for safari travel. As a national park, the Mara is extremely well preserved, but this also means that it is filled with a multitude of different camps—and, therefore, tourists—so travelers are rarely alone. The best way to experience Kenya is to go as remote as possible, and one of the beauties of Ol Malo is how exquisitely remote it is. On this privately owned property, visitors share the wildlife with nobody. There are so few places left in the world where one can be truly alone in nature.

The pet to have in Africa!

The Francombes help sustain a local school on their property, teaching children of all ages English, Swahili, and Samburu.

At Ol Malo, there is a program and workshop for Samburu women to assist them with working together on beaded items.

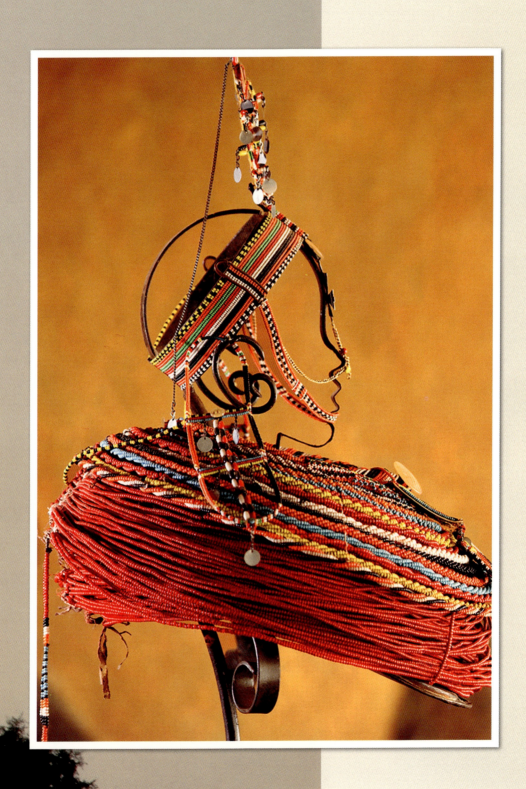

I'm better at communicating with horses.

Ol Malo sits on a five-thousand-acre parcel in Kenya's wild northern savannah on the Laikipia plateau, just beyond the foothills of Mount Kenya. The lodge itself is all open, with no windows or doors, so moving from room to room still gives the feeling of being at one with the surroundings. The architecture is very traditional and organic-feeling, created entirely with local woods, and the lobby's fireplace is hewn to look like a natural cave. Being in such a distant part of the world, I felt something magical—almost like everywhere I explored, I was the first person to stand where I was standing. One afternoon, we parked our Jeep in the middle of the savannah as innumerable elephants walked around us. To stay at Ol Malo is to live not just like a local, but to live like a very lucky local.

What began as a last-minute stopover at Ol Malo quickly turned into a monthlong sojourn, because my mother's friends are expert hosts and immediately welcomed me as one of their own. On some days, I would volunteer in the local Samburu school. On others, we would wake up early, go on safari, have breakfast on the savannah, and then drive around exploring all day. We would return home, freshen up, dress up in something a little smarter, and have long leisurely dinners in the fresh air, sipping wine and conversing late into the night, a million shining stars overhead in the sky. Having the Francombes as hosts made a world of difference. They might have been new friends when I arrived in Kenya, but by the time I left, we felt like old friends.

DON'T MISS

Explore the savannah through horseback riding, hiking, or, of course, safari. Come face-to-face with elephants, wild dogs, lions, zebras and monkeys—but keep an eye on the monkeys, because we learned the hard way that they will snatch up guests' breakfast when they aren't looking. And I didn't drink coffee at the time, but I do now—I will definitely be sampling the region's world-renowned coffee next time I'm in Kenya.

TOKYO, JAPAN
CARAVAN TOKYO

THE DISCOVERY

"Stretching out from the Meiji Shrine through the fashionable Harajuku and Aoyama districts, Omotesando is one of the world's greatest shopping avenues. Lined with highly designed, ultramodern office buildings and luxury retailers, it evokes a very specific vision of Tokyo, all polished glass and neon lighting. But that was not the Tokyo I was searching for. Although this district is filled with buildings designed by the world's best-known architects and teems with luxurious big-brand hotels, my husband had heard of a tiny caravan hidden in an alley somewhere off the main road—something at total odds with the aesthetic of the neighborhood, but something much closer to the heart of what Tokyo really is."

THE DESTINATION

The irony of staying in an Airstream parked in the middle of Japan's glossiest neighborhood is what makes Caravan Tokyo so charming. In a way, staying in one of these iconic midcentury all-American trailers is a very Japanese thing to do, with the unexpectedness, the camp, the sheer cuteness of it all. Caravan Tokyo is unassumingly tucked behind a few mixed-use office buildings, and its gray exterior blends in with the surroundings. But open the door and be greeted by a quirky interior: wood paneling, a pristine white bed, comforts like air-conditioning and reliable Wi-Fi, and a spacious shower. In short, it's all the space any traveling couple would need.

It is the position of Caravan Tokyo within the city, however, that makes it so special. Because guests are staying at ground level in a very pedestrian neighborhood, they feel much more connected to the pulse of the city; as opposed to being up in the clouds in one of the many high-rise hotels, they are actually on the ground and can spy on Tokyo's passersby going about their days. From the caravan's bed, we could see out the window and onto a beer garden and a juice bar—we enjoyed peeping on Tokyo's citizens scurrying off to their jobs in the morning, then sipping on Japanese beer at a nearby outdoor bar as the sun set after work.

Our Mexican host, a graphic designer who's been living in Tokyo for over a decade: He was wearing the typical Japanese souvenir jacket, but instead of being embroidered, it was hand painted.

DON'T MISS

An early-morning trip to the Tsukiji Fish Market to see locals exchange their fresh catch of the day, followed by a return to this neighborhood for dinner at any of the low-key, off-the-grid restaurants—no Michelin stars here, but the seafood is exceptional; exploring Kappabashi, the food utensil neighborhood where old chopsticks and cooking tools are laid to rest with a prayer of gratitude; seeing the priests in traditional garb at the Meiji Shrine, then shopping down Omotesando all the way back to Aoyama; and getting a Lolita makeover at Maison de Julietta before going for a walk on Takeshita Street.

ABOVE: I'm a firm believer in immersing myself in all types of fashion, and Lolita style is huge in Tokyo.
OPPOSITE: Three friends who collected vintage cars decided to refurbish an old caravan and make it the coolest room in Aoyama.

ISTANBUL, TURKEY

HAZZ

THE DISCOVERY

"Over the years, I have visited Istanbul four or five times—it is one of the only big cities in the world whose mysteries I enjoy rediscovering again and again. It is magical with an unfathomable amount of history, making the whole place come alive; even though the city dates back nearly three thousand years, its 'must-sees,' such as architecture, baths, and harems, never lose their charm. But I remember, my first time visiting, I felt as though I had not quite gotten to the core of what Istanbul is all about. I was in a touristic hotel near the Hagia Sophia, and I did not speak the language and found those ancient streets a bit difficult to navigate—and it didn't help that taxis regularly try to fake long drives to rip off unsuspecting visitors.

A couple of years later, I was explaining this to my friend Yaz Bukey, a Paris-based jewelry designer who is originally from Turkey, and she had the solution: The only place to stay in Istanbul, she said, is at Aslı Tunca's."

Every room at Aslı Tunca's has a distinct personality, each representing a different facet of this mysterious city.

Muesli, fresh apple juice, beautiful cutlery— the breakfast was so good and beautifully propped, I couldn't help but take a ton of pictures!

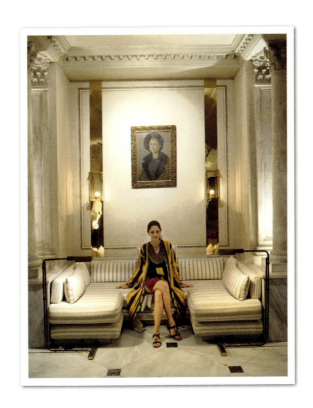

THE DESTINATION

From the outside, the house is shockingly plain. Nestled on a hushed, dignified block within the Beyoglu district across the water from the Topkapı Palace, one would never know from looking at the outside that this is a guesthouse owned by furniture designer Aslı Tunca and her husband, Carl Vercauteren, a Belgian sculptor. For thousands of years, the neighborhood has served as a crossroads for the different civilizations that have called Byzantium—then Constantinople, now Istanbul—home at different times: Byzantines, Greeks, Ottomans, French, British, and Italians. Tunca's home was built in the late 1800s, but during a recent renovation in the basement, she discovered the foundation of a much older home dating centuries back—every inch of this city oozes with secret histories. Tunca and Vercauteren call their little operation Hazz, from an old Turkish word for "enchantment."

Entering from the street, guests' eyes are treated to an aesthetic experience that only a designer-artist duo could deliver: austere gray Marmara marble floors and columns, gently faded chestnut wood on the stairs and walls, and luxurious Turkish linens upholstering the sofas and draped from the windows. Our pale green bedroom was done in warm woods, with a carved niche over the bed finished with the palest blush. The inspiration for the house's design pays homage to Istanbul's decorative culture, but the refinement and restraint reflects Tunca's European sensibilities.

ABOVE: Aslı's mother was a well-known beauty queen in her day, so everyone wanted to paint her. The house is filled with portraits of her done by famous artists.

The bookshelves are filled with Asli's inspiration binders. I spent the night flipping through, sneaking an inside peek at her creative process. The pale gray shelves themselves are absolutely gorgeous, too.

It is clear that Aslı is a woman of rarified and exquisite taste, but this becomes even more apparent when she steps foot outside the house. As I saw firsthand on an afternoon stroll with her, she moves through the streets of her neighborhood with a confidence and knowledge that only locals have, and she is on a first-name basis with all the best antiques dealers, every secret carpet shop, and the most splendid jewelers in the city. Seeing Istanbul through her eyes was like seeing an entirely different city from the one I had seen years before on my first trip. I finally felt that I had seen Istanbul for what it truly is—thecrossroads of the world, exotic in its history, and sumptuous to experience.

DON'T MISS

Today, when I visit Istanbul, although I still enjoy visiting those same tourist sites—the Topkapı Palace never gets old—I enjoy it even more when I can be spirited across the river to Aslı Tunca's impossibly elegant retreat. Her fresh homemade muesli and juices are better than anything found at a five-star hotel. Wander the streets and admire the layers of architecture accumulated over the millennia, and experience the thrills and mysteries of Istanbul in a funky way at any of the city's hidden "escape the room" puzzles—just pay attention at every sign and listen closely to instinct.

OPPOSITE, TOP: I will always remember the magical Istanbul nights we spent on the terrace with our hostess, talking about life over a bottle of wine.
BOTTOM: Aslı and her husband, artist Carl Vercauteren, furnished the entire home with furniture of their own design.

Visiting the harems and admiring the incredible tilework never gets old.

ABOVE, CENTER RIGHT: I invited Angie, my childhood friend, on a trip across Europe to take photographs.

PUGLIA, ITALY
MASSERIA POTENTI

THE DISCOVERY

"Every person has a different idea of what Italy is, but I have always been fascinated by the charms of Italian life in the countryside: sunshine, rolling hills, olive trees, fresh pasta hung out to dry.... My search brought me to the southeast, to Puglia, where this vision of la dolce vita *is alive and well."*

THE DESTINATION

For centuries, Puglia has been predominantly an agricultural region, producing nearly half of Italy's olive oil and much of its wine. Because of its distance from Rome, Milan, and the other major Italian cities, this heel of the Italian peninsula has largely managed to avoid too much tourism and development and remains an enchanting vision of idyllic pastoral Italy.

An estate of some 320 acres about three miles from the sea, the whitewashed stucco walls of Masseria Potenti date back to the sixteenth century. The structure itself is that of a classic Italian farm, with a rectangular main house surrounded by several low-lying wings and open-air walkways connecting the bedrooms to a central courtyard with a pool. It has passed through several families over the millennia, but today is a fully functioning farm and guesthouse owned by Maria Grazia di Lauro, the consummate Italian hostess and *madama* of the house. Like a true boss, she illuminates every room she occupies, and makes sure that every one of her guests is made to feel at home. Each room is a unique combination of warm pastel colors and rich Mediterranean hues, accented by pure white linens and filled with different antique furniture and nostalgic knickknacks.

The sprawling property was once owned by the Imperiali, one of Italy's most well known aristocratic families.

The rooms are so comfortable that visitors could spend all day in bed, but why would they? This is a farm, and there is work to be done! Maria Grazia loves when her guests show an interest in the farm work and will happily show them how to harvest grapes, olives, or fruit or help with the drying of herbs or the picking and jarring of vegetables. After all have earned their keep, so to speak, they are welcome to return to their bedrooms for a long, lazy nap or pull up a chaise by the pool and soak up the rest of the afternoon.

At sunset, every guest gathers around the common table to enjoy dinner alfresco. There is no menu at Masseria Potenti, so everyone is treated to a lavish spread of whichever fresh fruit, vegetables, and meats Maria Grazia found at market that day. I'm still dreaming about the slightly tart, impossibly succulent cherry tomatoes on *friselle* bread sprinkled with olive oil and fresh oregano.

DON'T MISS

Asking Maria Grazia for some dried herbs, homemade sauces, and vegetables in oil to bring home; taking an afternoon trip to Lecce to stroll freely and admire the baroque architecture in the absence of crowds; driving to the nearby village of Grottaglie, famous for its pottery; and best of all, stepping off the property for a quiet walk through fields of fragrant wild rosemary.

Guests who enjoy farming are invited to help with the harvest.

A place where one arrives with the enthusiasm for discovery and leaves with the yearning to return.

Directory

AFRICA

BOTSWANA

Jack's Camp
Adventure waits around every turn at this campsite, including in the library, where guests can learn about legendary explorers and African wildlife.
Makgadikgadi Pan, Botswana
+27 11 326 4407
unchartedafrica.com
reservations@unchartedafrica.com

KIWAYU, KENYA

Aman Lamu
A boutique of beachwear styles created by the stylish and beautiful Sandy Bornman.
Lamu, Kenya
sandybornman@gmail.com

Mike's Camp
This remote camp is run by Mike himself, whose encyclopedic knowledge of the wilderness makes him the ideal host.
Kiwayu, Lamu, Kenya
+254 718 004 920
mikescampkiwayu.com
enquiries@mikescampkiwayu.com

Peponi Hotel
The Korschen family opened this hotel in 1967, and its twenty-eight ocean-view rooms retain their original charm.
Shela, Kenya
+254 722 203 082
peponi-lamu.com
reservation@peponi-lamu.com

LAIKIPIA, KENYA

Ol Malo
Owned and run by the Francombe family, this 5,000-acre ranch is the perfect destination for those looking for both wildlife and privacy—no other visitors will be there.
Laikipia, Kenya
+254 721 630 686
olmalo.com
info@olmalo.com

MARRAKECH, MOROCCO

Beldi
This clothing boutique, owned by two brothers, always has the newest westernized Moroccan fashions for men and women.
9-11 Soukiat Laksour
Marrakesh, Morocco
+212 5244 41076

Jardin Majorelle
A delightful twelve-acre garden, filled with exotic flora and bubbling streams, that took French painter Jacques Majorelle forty years to complete.
Rue Yves Saint Laurent
Marrakech 40090, Morocco
+212 5243 13047
jardinmajorelle.com

Jemaa el-Fna
This main square of Marrakech is a bustling center whose name is often interpreted to mean "The Mosque at the End of the World."
Square of Marrakech
Marrakech 40000, Morocco

La Mamounia
This palace hotel, opened in 1923, was named after Prince Al Mamoun, who received its gardens as a wedding gift.
Avenue Bab Jdid
Marrakech 40040, Morocco
+212 5243 88600
mamounia.com
informations@mamounia.com

Le Foundouk
Located in the souks of Marrakech and previously a warehouse, this restaurant, restored in 2000, boasts a panoramic terrace overlooking the Medina.
55, Souk Hal Fassi Kaat Bennahïd, Medina
Marrakech 40000, Morocco
+ 212 5243 78190
foundouk.com
contact@foundouk.com

Le Grand Café de la Poste
French cuisine with Mediterranean accents in the heart of Guéliz.
Avenue Imam Malik
Marrakech 40000, Morocco
+212 5244 33038

Riad Jardin Secret
Cyrielle and Julien's riad is built in the "anti-modern" style, embracing the imperfections that come with the passing of time.
43-46 Arset Aouzal
Marrakech 40000, Morocco
+212 5243 76606
riadjardinsecret.com
contact@riadjardinsecret.com

ASIA

KYOTO, JAPAN

B. B-Peak Snack
Kyoto is not always welcoming to foreigners—most bars are "Japanese only"—but you will be allowed into this secret karaoke bar, although you'll likely be the only one from out of town.
Gion, Kyoto, Japan
+81 75 525 0552

El Coyote
Kyoto's colorful version of Latin dining and dancing.
Wisteria Court Pontocho B1F
Ishiya Town
604-8002 Kyoto, Japan
+81 75 231 1527
el-coyote.com

Geisha Makeover
Lucky travelers will be able to spot real geishas walking around Kyoto, but they can also get their own makeovers and play the role themselves for the day. Don't miss a walk in the Bamboo Grove in Maiko attire!
4-10 Sagatenryuuji
Tateishichou, Ukyou
616-8375 Kyoto, Japan

Midnight Cafe 528
Hidden on the fifth floor of a nondescript building, this tiny eight-seat bar is owned and run by a young Japanese singer with a great CD collection of blues and jazz.
Gion, Kyoto, Japan
+81 75 741 8461

Shigaraki Pottery Village
A peaceful town an hour away from Kyoto, steeped in the rich history of Japanese pottery.
1131 Nagano
Koka 529-1851
Shiga Prefecture, Japan

Sobanomi Yoshimura
This delicious, authentic Soba restaurant is perfect for lunch— ask for a table in the back room, where the locals eat.
3-5 Sagatenryuji Susukinobabacho
Ukyo, Kyoto 616-8385, Japan
+81 75 353 0114

Tawara-ya Ryokan
Run by the same family for three centuries, this inn is an icon of Kyoto's history.
278 Nakahakusancho
Gion, Nakagyo
Kyoto 604-8094, Japan
+81 75 211 5566

SHIKOKU, JAPAN

Ikadaya
Private dining, where seafood is served aboard a raft.
4496 Shitaba, Uwajima
Ehime Prefecture, Japan
+81 895 29 0831

Kiya Ryokan
This ryokan stunningly captures the style of Japan's nineteenth-century Meiji period.
2-8-2 Honmachioute
Uwajima-shi, Ehime-ken
798-0041 Shikoku, Japan
+81 895 22 0101
kiyaryokan.com
contact@kiyaryokan.com

TOKYO, JAPAN

Caravan Tokyo
Parked among the cutting-edge architecture of Tokyo's central Aoyama neighborhood, this caravan is a charming midcentury escape.
3-13 Commune 246
Minato-ku, Minato-Aoyama
Tokyo, Japan
+81 90 3247 1413
caravantokyo.com

Maison de Julietta
Lolita is not a trend or a costume: It's a fashion, and for those who want to try it, Maison de Julietta offers the perfect makeovers.
Harajuku, 1 Chome-11-6, Laforet Jingumae, Shibuya
150-0001 Tokyo, Japan
+81 36 434 5464
maison-de-julietta.com

Mandarake Shibuya Anime Store
A haven for fans of Japanese pop culture, Mandarake Shibuya is one of the world's largest anime and manga stores.
Udagawacho, 31-2
Shibuya, 150-0042 Tokyo, Japan
+81 33 477 0777

EUROPE

KASTELLORIZO, GREECE

Alexandra's Restaurant
Fresh seafood and the Papoutsi family's excellent service make Alexandra's unforgettable.
Kastellorizo, Greece
+30 2246 049019

Faros Cafe
A morning dive while waiting for coffee at Faros is the perfect way to start the day.
85111 Kastellorizo, Greece
+30 2246 049509

Lazarakis
The kind of place to return to for breakfast, lunch, and dinner.
Kastellorizo 85111, Greece
+30 2246 049370

Mediterraneo Megisti
French architect Marie Rivalant's light design touches and cheerful disposition illuminate this hotel.
851 11, Kastelorizo, Greece
+30 2246 049007
mediterraneo-megisti.com
bookings@mediterraneo-kastelorizo.com

Radio Cafe
The ideal spot for breakfast and sundowners, where owners Elma and Vangelis are always around making sure every plate comes out fresh and fast.
Kastellorizo, Greece
+30 2246 049029

Ta Platania
This little family-run tavern serves homemade food with a smile.
Kastellorizo 85111, Greece
+30 2246 049206

PATMOS, GREECE

Archontariki
A prime example of elegant Aegean architecture, this hotel offers suites with the themes of Wisdom, Joy, Hope, Love, and Faith.
Chora, Patmos 85500, Greece
+30 2247 029368
archontariki.co.uk
info@archontariki-patmos.gr

Niko's
This tiny eatery, along a secluded beach road, offers beautiful sunset views, fried fish, and fresh water—the ideal stop on the way back from the beach.
Patmos, Greece

Pantheon
Located at the entrance to Chora, this restaurant has the best octopus.
+30 2247 031226
Chora, Patmos 85500, Greece

RHODES, GREECE

Marco Polo Mansion
The magic of the Marco Polo is amplified by the owner's artworks in progress, which can be found all over the mansion.
Agiou Fanouriou 40-42
Rhodes 85100, Greece
+30 2241 025562
marcopolomansion.gr
marcopolomansion@hotmail.com

Nireas
A fish restaurant at the back of the ancient city, apart from the crowds.
Sofokleous 22
Rhodes 85100, Greece
+30 2241 021703

SYMI, GREECE

Old Markets, Symi
What was formerly a cluster of historical shops is now a luxurious property furnished with silver once owned by King George I of Greece.
Kali Strata, Ano
Symi 85600, Greece
+30 2246 071440
theoldmarkets.com
info@theoldmarkets.com

Soroco
This lifestyle store in Symi offers an exquisite selection of products such as baskets, kitchenware, and rope sandals.
Symi 85600, Greece
+30 22460 71002
soroco.gr
shop@soroco.gr

ICELAND

Hótel Búðir
This hotel sits on a lava field at the edge of the Snaefellsnes peninsula in west Iceland and offers breathtaking views of the nearby glacier and estuary.
356 Snæfellsbær
Iceland
+354 435 6700
hotelbudir.is
budir@budir.is

Hótel Flatey
On a remote island, unparalleled serenity abounds at Hótel Flatey, which is open from late May to early September.
Flatey, 300 Flatey, Iceland
+354 555 7788
hotelflatey.is
info@hotelflatey.is

Thrihnukagigur Volcano
The only volcano on earth that can be explored on the inside!
Iceland
+354 519 5609
insidethevolcano.com/the-volcano
info@insidethevolcano.com

NAPLES, ITALY

Albergo del Purgatorio
Nathalie de Saint Phalle welcomes travelers to their own 4,000-square-foot apartment in a fabulously decadent palazzo.
Palazzo Marigliano 39
Via San Biagio dei Librai
80138 Naples, Italy
+39 081 299 579
nhsp@aol.com

Cappella Sansevero
This chapel, built in 1590, houses the famous Veiled Christ, known for the remarkable tissue-like quality of its marble.
Via Francesco De Sanctis, 19/21
80134 Naples, Italy
+39 081 551 8470
museosansevero.it
info@museosansevero.it

Camiceria Piccolo
Made-to-measure shirts since 1926, expertly tailored by the Piccolo family.
Via Chiaia, 41
80132 Naples, Italy
+39 081 411824
camiceriapiccolo.com

Da Dora
Founded in 1973 by a couple, both of whom came from families of fishermen, this restaurant prides itself on its fresh seafood.
Via Ferdinando Palasciano, 28
80122 Naples, Italy
+39 081 680519
ristorantedora.it
info@ristorantedora.it

Di Matteo
Visualize the epitome of a Neapolitan pizzeria—this place looks just like it.
Via dei Tribunali, 94
80138 Naples, Italy
+39 081 455262

Gay Odin
Exquisite Neapolitan chocolate, crafted by artisans.
Via Vetriera, 12
80100 Naples, Italy
gay-odin.it
shop@gayodin.it

Museo Archeologico Nazionale
Naples's National Archaeological Museum harbors artifacts from Pompeii, Stabiae, and Herculaneum.
Piazza Museo, 19
80135 Naples, Italy
+39 081 442 2149
cir.campania.beniculturali.it/museoarcheologiconazionale

POSITANO, ITALY

Amatruda
This paper mill and the Amatruda family's tradition and technique date back to the fifteenth century.
Via delle Cartiere, 100
84011 Amalfi
Salerno, Italy
+39 089 871315
amatruda.it/en/amatruda-paper-mill
info@amatruda.it

Da Adolfo
For excellent mussels and mozzarella in Positano, look for Adolfo's boat topped with a wooden fish painted red.
**Via Laurito, 40
84017 Positano SA, Italy
+39 089 875022**
daadolfo.com
info@daadolfo.com

Hotel Le Sirenuse
Filled with antiques hand-picked by the Sersale family, Le Sirenuse is a family-owned and -run gem.
**Via Cristoforo Colombo, 30
84017 Positano, Italy
+39 089 875066**
sirenuse.it
info@sirenuse.it

La Bottega di Brunella
This linen atelier creates clothing, beachwear, and accessories suitable for a dolce vita holiday.
**Via Pasitea, 72
Positano, SA 84017, Italy
+39 089 875228**
abbigliamentopositanobrunella.com

Le Tre Sorelle
Located right by Positano's colorful beach, this traditional restaurant is a must for mussel pasta.
**Via del Brigantino, 27/29
84017 Positano SA, Italy
+39 089 875452**

Lo Scoglio da Tommaso
This restaurant's zucchini pasta is worth the thirty-minute boat ride from Positano.
**Piazza delle Sirene, 15
Marina del Cantone, Massa Lubrense
Naples, Italy
+39 081 808 1026**
hotelloscoglio.com
info@hotelloscoglio.com

Parco dei Principi
Architect Gio Ponti constructed this iconic hotel in 1959 on the site of a dacha meant for Tsar Nicholas II.
**Via Bernardino Rota, 44
80067 Sorrento NA, Italy
+39 081 878 4644**
royalgroup.it/parcodeiprincipi
info@hotelparcoprincipi.com

Villa TreVille
The four villas—Bianca, Azzurra, Rosa, and Tre Pini—were named and decorated by director Franco Zeffirelli, who discovered the property in 1941.
**Via Arienzo, 30
84017 Positano SA, Italy
+39 089 812 2411**
villatreville.com
info@villatreville.com

PUGLIA, ITALY

Masseria Potenti
Maria Grazia di Lauro is the welcoming hostess of this serene farm and guesthouse.
**Contrada Potenti
74024 Manduria TA, Italy
+39 099 973 5408**
masseriapotenti.it
info@masseriapotenti.it

MALLORCA, SPAIN

Ca Na Toneta
Sisters Maria and Teresa Solivellas set each table of their homey restaurant with the best of the island's fresh local produce, cooking with techniques and recipes inspired by local traditions.
**Carrer de s'Horitzó, 21
07314 Caimari, Mallorca, Spain
+34 971 51 52 26**
canatoneta.com
info@canatoneta.com

Cala Deià
Straight out of a movie from the sixties, this rocky beach is perfect for lunch by the sea.
Deià, Mallorca, Spain

Consell Flea Market
On Sunday mornings, barter with sellers for anything from elegant vintage furniture to hand-painted dresses.
**Plaça Major, 3
07330 Consell, Mallorca, Spain
+34 971 62 20 95**

Gerreria Pere Coll
Visit for Mallorca's best handmade ceramics.
**Calle de Cals Ollers 23
Pòrtol, Marratxí, Spain
+34 971 60 27 46**
ollersdeportol.com
gerreriaperecoll@msn.com

Sa Foradada
Make sure to indulge in the paella at this special restaurant, which is best reachable by boat.
**Diseminado Sa Foradada, 2
07179 Deià, Mallorca, Spain
+34 616 08 74 99**
saforadada.com

Sa Palosa
Chaime and Jorge are the heart and soul of this retreat, which includes yoga, vegetarian food, and panoramic sunsets.
**Sóller, Mallorca, Spain
+ 34 653 806 565**
jaime@sopa.vg
jorge@sopa.vg

Santa Maria Market
Fresh fruit and vegetables on Sundays from 9 a.m. to 2 p.m.
Santa Maria del Camí, Mallorca, Spain

POSCHIAVO, SWITZERLAND

La Rösa
Located at the Bernina Pass, connecting Italy to Switzerland, this renovated post office makes an elegant hotel.
**CH-7742 La Rösa, Valposchiavo
7742 Poschiavo, Switzerland
+ 41 81 832 60 51**
larosa.ch
mail@larosa.ch

Museo Casa Console
This museum documents Italian contemporary art from the 1980s to today, highlighting the artist colony formed by Emilio Scanavino.
**Via da Mez 32
7742 Poschiavo, Switzerland
+41 81 844 00 40**
museocasaconsole.ch
info@museocasaconsole.ch

ISTANBUL, TURKEY

Hazz
Furniture designer Aslı Tunca hosts guests at her impeccably decorated home.
**Tomtom, Nur-i Ziya Sk. 34/20
34433 Beyoglu, Istanbul, Turkey
+90 212 251 70 57
aslitunca.com
info@aslitunca.com**

Papilio
This textile shop in the Grand Bazaar has a vast and beautiful selection of linen and cotton.
**+90 242 836 28 95
Uzunçarsı, Kas, Turkey**

Topkapı Palace
A main residence of the Ottoman sultans for over 400 years.
**Cankurtaran Mh., 34122 Fatih
Istanbul, Turkey
+90 212 512 04 80
topkapisarayi.gov.tr
topkapisarayimuzesi@kulturturizm.gov.tr**

Unlock
An escape room where visitors must solve puzzles to leave!
**Tomtom, New Market Street No. 26/9
Beyoglu, Istanbul, Turkey
+90 212 232 86 17
unlock.com.tr
info@unlock.com.tr**

The Works, "Objects of Desire"
A unique museum, gallery, and antique shop.
**Kuloglu Mah. Faik Pasa Cad. No. 6/1
Beyoglu, Istanbul, Turkey
+90 532 245 16 73
karacaborar@gmail.com**

NORTH AMERICA

HARBOUR ISLAND, BAHAMAS

Angela's Starfish Restaurant
The conch salad is the best choice.
**Dunmore Town
Harbour Island, Bahamas
+1 242 333 2253**

Ocean View Club
Founded by Pip and now managed by her son Ben and his wife, Charlie, this guesthouse is the coziest place on the island.
**Gaol Lane, Dunmore Town
Harbour Island, Bahamas
+1 242 333 2276
ilovetheoceanview.com
reserve.oceanview@gmail.com**

The Landing
Thirteen guest rooms designed in classic plantation style with colonial-inspired Caribbean influences.
**Bay Street
Harbour Island, The Bahamas
+1 242 333 2707
harbourislandlanding.com
thelanding@coralwave.com**

YUCATÁN, MEXICO

Hacienda San Jose
Stay in a *palapa* for a true Mayan experience, or dine at the hacienda's restaurant for cuisine designed around the property's orchards.
**KM 30 Carretera
97470 Tixkokob, Yucatán, Mexico
+52 999 924 1333
haciendasanjosecholul.com
thehaciendas@luxurycollection.com**

Hacienda Santa Rosa
This elegant hacienda enchants the senses, from private plunge pools to striking embroidery to flowery scents.
**Carretera Mérida Campeche
97800 Santa Rosa, Yucatán, Mexico
+52 999 923 1923
haciendasantarosa.com
thehaciendas@luxurycollection.com**

Hacienda Temozon
Surrounded by a lush tropical rain forest, this hotel is an ideal getaway for nature lovers.
**KM 182 Carretera Merida-Uxmal
97825 Temozon Sur, Yucatán, Mexico
+52 999 923 8089
haciendatemozon.com
thehaciendas@luxurycollection.com**

SOUTH AMERICA

MENDOZA, ARGENTINA

Finca Los Alamos
The 12,000 acres of this picturesque property are covered with vineyards and orchards. Visitors can create a personalized barrel of wine and try to convince Carolina, the owner and manager, to host them for a couple of nights at her historical home.
**Bariloche, Confluencia
Calle Bombal Sin Numero
San Rafael 5600, Mendoza, Argentina
+54 26 0463 8780
bombalyaldao.com.ar**

PATAGONIA, ARGENTINA

Los Ombues Lodge
A destination for hunters who long to hunt duck, partridge, and dove on the same sprawling property.
**Entre Ríos, Argentina
+54 34 3642 4285
losombues.com
info@losombues.com**

Estancia Arroyo Verde
Choose between one of the four rooms in the main house or forgo electricity to stay at the log cabin atop a rocky outcrop overlooking Lake Traful.
**Bariloche, Confluencia
Patagonia, Argentina
+54 11 4801 7448
estanciaarroyoverde.com.ar
info@estanciaarroyoverde.com.ar**

Hosteria Las Balsas
This hotel's vibrant blue facade is an iconic part of the view over Kraft Bay.
Cabellera de la Berenice 445, Q8407ZCA
Villa La Angostura
Neuquén, Argentina
+54 294 449 4308
lasbalsas.com
info@lasbalsas.com.ar

Tinto Bistro
Argentinian cuisine prepared with European flair.
Nahuel Huapi 34
Villa La Angostura
Neuquén, Argentina
+54 294 449 4924

TRANCOSO, BRAZIL

Uxua Casa Hotel & Spa
Each of Uxua's rooms, designed and curated by Wilbert Das, is adorned with handmade furniture and original artwork.
Porto Seguro, Trancoso
45810 Bahia, Brazil
+55 73 3668 2277
uxua.com
info@uxua.com

GARZÓN, URUGUAY

Casa Anna
Martin and Annie Summers let guests rent out their six idyllic casitas, surrounded by gardens and a pool.
Garzón, Uruguay
+598 4410 2800
casaannagarzon.com
info@restaurantegarzon.com

Garzon
A restaurant and hotel by prominent Argentinan chef Francis Mallmann.
Costa Jose Ignacio, 20401
Garzón, Maldonado Department, Uruguay
+598 4410 2809
restaurantegarzon.com
info@restaurantegarzon.com

Lucifer
Six tables and pastel chairs are the setting for a menu that changes daily.
20401 Garzón
Maldonado Department, Uruguay
+598 9925 5249
lucifer.com.uy
lucifer@lucifer.com.uy

Medialunas Calentitas
Unparalleled croissants and other baked goods.
21 de Setiembre 2982
La Barra
11300 Montevideo Department, Uruguay
+598 4277 2347
medialunascalentitas.com

Parador La Caracola
Fresh, delicious food at a restaurant accessible only by boat—and by invitation.
Los Tilos y Los Malvones
20306 Balneario Las Flores
Maldonado Department, Uruguay
+598 9422 3015
paradorlacaracola.com
reservas@paradorlacaracola.com

Parador La Huella
Dulce de leche volcanoes are La Huella's delicious claim to fame.
Calle de Los Cisnes, 20402
José Ignacio
Maldonado Department, Uruguay
+598 4486 2279
paradorlahuella.com
info@paradorlahuella.com

ACKNOWLEDGMENTS

A special thanks to my indomitable mother, Maita Barrenechea, who made me a curious explorer and bestowed on me my passion for discovery.

Eternal gratitude to my loving husband and best travel buddy, Alex de Betak, who encourages me to pursue each and every wild dream. I could not ask for a better life companion, one who even loves seeing and eating the same things as me every time.

Thank you to my right hand, my friend, and my *pollito*, Marti Arcucci, whom I cannot live without.

Thank you to the fabulous Todd Plummer, who helped put my messy memories into charming words and proper paragraphs.

Thank you to my sister Lucia Sanchez Barrenechea for illustrating the beautiful map in this book. Thank you to my other sister Catu Sanchez Barrenechea for always being there for me and helping me put this book together.

Lots of thank-yous to my family and friends, who give me the strength and support I need despite the distance.

Thank you to Amael and Aidyn for always joining us on these trips and reminding us how to see the world with kids' eyes.

Thank you very much to all those who generously shared some special places with me: Waris Ahluwalia, Laura Bailey, Yaz Bukey, Isabella Capece, Vincent Darré, Alber Elbaz, Dorian Grinspan, Alex Koo, Caroline de Maigret, Isabel Marant, Camille Miceli, Carlos Mota, Felipe Oliveira Baptista, Gaia Repossi, Nicoletta Santoro, Princess Elisabeth von Thurn und Taxis, Elie Top, and especially Paola Corini and Laura Taccari, cofounders of *Meraviglia Paper*. Thank you all for showing me there are more people like us out there, who value these understated gems more than any number of stars.

Thanks to Isaias Miciu for capturing the celestial magic of our beloved Patagonia with such sophisticated ease. Thank you to Angie Holmberg for taking such gorgeous pictures during our Hellenic adventures.

Merci beaucoup to the entire Assouline team for their patience and dedication, and for believing in me on this very special quest.

Last and most important, thank you to all the warm hosts who open their homes to us visitors and make us feel like good old friends. It takes a lot of energy and a lot of love to make a house feel like a home.

Assouline would like to thank AltaImage and Barbara Gogan for their invaluable contributions to this book.

CREDITS

All images © Sofía Sanchez de Betak except the following: Pages 7, 11, 14 (except top left), 15 (top), 28, 29 (except bottom right), 36–37, 49 (top), 55 (bottom right), 56 (bottom), 59 (bottom), 65–67, 70–71 (center), 78 (bottom left), 79 (bottom), 92 (bottom left), 93 (bottom), 96, 106 (top), 109 (bottom right), 113 (center), 122 (bottom right), 128 (bottom left), 132 (bottom left), 136 (center right), 153 (bottom), 154 (bottom right), 155 (top left and right and bottom right), 166–67, 170 (top left and right), 176 (top and bottom background), 177: © Alexandre de Betak; pages 12–13, 14 (top left), 15 (except top), 16, 18–25, 68, 70–71 (except center), 73–75, 76–77 (except top right), 137 (except top), 138–39, 142 (except background), 151–52, 153 (except bottom), 155 (center and bottom left), 168–69, 170 (bottom), 171–75, 176 (top left and bottom): © Angeles Holmberg; page 27 (background): © kromka/Shutterstock.com; pages 33–35: © Laura Taccari; page 39: © Marina Larivière; pages 40, 42–45, 111–12, 114–15: © Isaias Miciu; pages 43 (top left and right), 159 (bottom right): © Maita Barrenechea; pages 47–48, 49 (except top), 50–51: © Cyrielle Astaing; page 59 (top): © Mike's Camp; page 79 (top left): © Old Markets, Symi; pages 81–82, 83 (except top right): © Omote Nobutada; page 83 (background): © My name is boy/Shutterstock.com; pages 95, 97 (except center left): © Marriott International, Inc.; page 100: © Uncharted Africa Safari Co.; pages 101–105, 106–107, 109 (except bottom right): © Luca De Santis for Jack's Camp; page 109 (background): © DiversityStudio/Shutterstock.com; pages 117–18, 119 (except center right), 120–21, 122 (except bottom right), 123: © Fernando Lombardi; page 125 (top left): © Martina Arcucci; page 131 (top): © Linda Fargo; page 131 (bottom): © Natalie Joos; page 132, 133: © Martin Summers; pages 145, 147 (right), 148 (except bottom left), 149: © Luisa Zuberbuhler; page 145 (background): © yoshi0511/Shutterstock.com; page 145 (top right): © Sergio Sandona; page 158 (except bottom right), 163: © Ol Malo; page 161: © Samburu Trust; pages 179–81, 182 (except bottom), 183–85: © Masseria Potenti.

Every possible effort has been made to identify and contact all rightsholders and obtain their permission for work appearing on these pages. Any errors and omissions brought to the publisher's attention will be corrected in future editions.